YOU'VE GOT IT MADE

ALSO BY MARIAN BURROS

Keep It Simple: 30-Minute Meals from Scratch

Pure & Simple: Delicious Recipes for Additive-Free Cooking

Elegant but Easy

Freeze with Ease

Come for Cocktails, Stay for Supper

The Summertime Cookbook

YOU'VE GOT IT MADE

Marian Burros

WILLIAM MORROW AND COMPANY, INC.

New York 1984

Library of Congress Catalog Card Number: 84-60444

ISBN: 0-688-03187-0

Printed in the United States of America

BOOK DESIGN BY BETTY BINNS GRAPHICS/MARTIN LUBIN

CONTENTS

ACKNOWLEDGMENTS

It's customary to acknowledge people who have been supportive of an author when she is writing a book. Often spouses are included simply because they have had to put up with a cranky mate. My husband, Donald, however, has contributed more than just his patience. As he always has in the past, he continues to contribute his taste buds. If he thinks a dish "doesn't have it," as he says, he never minces words. It makes my work a lot easier.

Particular thanks to Linda Smith, too. Linda is a registered dietician with Public Voice for Food & Health Policies in Washington, D.C. She calculated the nutritional value for all the family menus and always had a good suggestion on how to achieve the right balance between taste and nutrition.

To my tester, taster, consultant and friend, Shang Patterson, my deepest appreciation, especially for her work under deadline pressures.

And finally to my editor, Maria Guarnaschelli, thank you for improving my prose; to my agent, Ann Buchwald, thank you for keeping my spirits up.

Marian Burros
Bethesda, Maryland
January, 1984

INTRODUCTION

You've Got It Made was written for everyone who prepares the family dinner and doesn't stay home all day to do it, and for people who have been forced to give up entertaining at home because they no longer want to spend three days cooking and cleaning for a party.

It's not a book for people who have maids or cooks, who can afford to have their parties catered, or who eat out every night. That leaves about 99 percent of the population.

The recipes in the book are divided into two sections: family meals that are quick and easy for one person to prepare alone or with some assistance, and dinner parties to which all the guests bring a dish under the direction of the host or hostess.

This book is an amalgamation of two of the previous books I wrote, *Pure & Simple,* subtitled *Delicious Recipes for Additive-Free Cooking,* and *Keep It Simple,* subtitled *30-Minute Meals from Scratch,* but all the recipes are new.

The central idea of the forty-five menus in the family meal section of this new book is to keep dinner preparation under thirty minutes without using convenience foods. This has been accomplished using two different techniques: There are thirty menus in which the main dishes have been made ahead and frozen. These are marked (F) in the recipe titles and in the recipe list preceding that introduction. There are fifteen menus, based on the same premise as *Keep It Simple,* simplification of the recipes so that the entire meal can be prepared in thirty minutes. The latter meals have been included because the concept proved so successful the first time.

For many people, however, the desire to do the bulk of the work in advance, on the weekend when there is more uninterrupted time, is even greater. Weekend cooking for the following work week has become something of a ritual, especially in families where both heads of the household work. It is often engaged in by more than one family member. With two people cooking, preparing dinner turns into a breeze. One Saturday a friend and I were in the kitchen from 9 A.M. to 4 P.M., and we produced thirteen different dishes!

During the week these frozen treasures are taken out and defrosted the night before they are to be served. Then, at dinner, one or two suggested side dishes are put together in five to fifteen minutes, while the main dish is heating.

7

These menus offer a welcome relief from the all too familiar quick fix—
the fattening, oversalted, tasteless TV dinners, prepared mixes and carry-
out food. But if I tell you these meals are also good for you, will you balk?

Since nutrition has become a vital concern in modern life, I thought
that people who are interested in this book would want to know that the
family meals are based on Dietary Guidelines for the United States and the
National Academy of Sciences dietary guidelines based on their 1982 report
"Diet, Nutrition and Cancer."

In gustatory terms that means the servings of vegetables and starches
are larger than they normally are at the American table while the servings of
meat, fish and poultry are smaller. It also means that no salt is added;
instead, the seasonings come from an extensive use of herbs and spices.

When one of the foremost French chefs, Alain Senderens, says health
and good food are synonymous, skeptics should be convinced. M. Senderens
was referring to the kind of food he prepares at his three-star Parisian
restaurant, L'Archestrate: "Fast cooking to hold the vitamins and minerals in
the food; raw or slightly cooked vegetables and fish; fewer sauces."

M. Senderens went on to say in an interview with Richard E. Kann in
Caterer and Hotelkeeper, an English publication, "We must pay attention to the
female customer, who is very concerned with keeping a slim figure while still
eating well. This certainly means we must watch the fattening dishes
carefully."

M. Senderens apparently came to these conclusions because he has
noticed that "people are beginning to understand about eating differently
. . . for the taste and for health reasons. The evolution is particularly
noticeable among the young. More than seventy-five percent of my present
customers are connoisseurs," he said.

If that style of cooking is good enough for such a talented and
imaginative chef, it should be good enough for us.

If you decide you wish to follow the dietary guidelines for the entire
day, I have tried to make it easier by offering the calorie count, percent of
fat and amount of sodium and fiber in each of the dinner menus.

The party recipes are a different matter. There is no nutrition
information because I feel very strongly that if you eat judiciously five or six
days a week, you can splurge on the weekend.

Menus for entertaining are not, however, the standard I-must-spend-every-
waking-minute-before-next-week's-party-preparing-for-it. Instead, they are
recipes to be made by the host or hostess and friends. They are the present-tense
version of covered-dish suppers or potluck, except that there is nothing potluck
about them because the person hosting the party arranges them to prevent a table
bedecked with three macaroni-and-cheese casseroles.

And everyone brings something: Those who can't cook bring the wine
or liquor. The menus and recipes can be used either to organize your own
cooperative dinner or to provide you with lots of ideas on what to bring if
you are asked to contribute to one. There is a third way they can be used as

well. If just two of you want to give a dinner together, you can divide the work as a friend and I have been doing for the last twelve years for New Year's Eve.

But before you get to the recipes, perhaps you would like to know why the family meals are based on "Dietary Guidelines for the United States" and the National Academy of Sciences report "Diet, Nutrition and Cancer." The next chapter attempts to answer that question. It may also convince you about the desirability of cooking at home.

Armed with that information, with simplified methods for getting family meals on the table in less than half an hour and for having friends in for dinner, wouldn't you agree that *You've Got It Made?*

THE POLITICS OF DIETARY GUIDELINES

If Americans are confused about what they should be eating, they have a perfect right to be. Advertisements and commercials implore us to choose foods loaded with fat, salt and sugar—Hostess doughnuts for breakfast, potato chips between lunch and dinner and Coke anytime. One set of nutritionists tells us to cut out those foods while another, admittedly a much smaller, group tells us they won't do any harm. And our doctors tell us nothing.

Bewildered and exasperated, most of us have chosen to follow a little of everyone's advice, hoping we've got the right mix. Otherwise how can you explain these schizophrenic eating patterns between 1976 and 1981?*

Soft drink consumption up from 392 twelve-ounce servings per capita to 412.5.

Coffee consumption down from 690 six-ounce cups to 567.3 cups.

Beef consumption down from 97.8 pounds to 78.8 pounds.

Pork consumption up from 54.6 pounds to 65 pounds.

Chicken consumption up from 42.7 pounds to 51.7 pounds.

What's more, we are drinking more low-fat milk and less whole milk, eating more margarine and less butter. But our overall fat consumption is 34 percent higher than it was in 1910 and the amount of complex carbohydrates (fruits, vegetables and whole grains) we consume is down 43 percent since 1910.

In the days when the federal government thought it was a good idea to help people make good nutritional choices, it offered some advice for sorting out all the conflicting information in a small pamphlet called "Dietary Guidelines for the United States." It was published in February 1980. The Guidelines made the following seven very simple and very generalized suggestions:

Eat a variety of foods.

Maintain ideal weight.

Avoid too much fat, saturated fat and cholesterol.

* "The Changing American Diet," Center for Science in the Public Interest.

Eat foods with adequate starch and fiber.

Avoid too much sugar.

Avoid too much sodium.

If you drink alcohol, do so in moderation.

The Guidelines are based on the theory that many diseases of the Western world are the result of improper eating and that the quality of life can be improved through proper nutrition. Being in favor of them would seem to be about as controversial as speaking out for Mom and apple pie.

But when the Reagan administration took office in January 1981, the government went out of the advice business for humans and concentrated instead on cutting food out of the diet altogether for people unfortunate enough to need food stamps or the WIC (Women, Infants and Children Supplemental Feeding) Program. The administration has stopped the free distribution of Dietary Guidelines and programs designed to implement the Guidelines, in response to pressure from certain segments of the food industry, particularly meat, dairy and egg producers. Even so, they have been unable to reverse the impact of the eight million copies that have already been distributed.

A brief tour of the path traveled by Dietary Guidelines since the day their predecessor report, "Dietary Goals for the United States," was released in January 1977 offers a bit of insight into how even good nutrition can become a political football. To those who wonder what could possibly be political about food—read on.

When the Senate Select Committee on Nutrition and Human Needs announced the Dietary Goals, large segments of the food industry, along with a few scientists, rushed forward to denounce them.

These are the changes they denounced:

An increase of complex carbohydrate consumption to account for 55 to 60 percent of caloric intake, by increasing consumption of fruits, vegetables and whole grains.

Reduction of overall fat consumption, from approximately 40 percent to 30 percent, by decreasing consumption of meat and increasing consumption of poultry and fish.

Reduction of saturated fat consumption to account for about 10 percent of total calories; balanced with polyunsaturated and monosaturated fats, which should account for about 10 percent of calories each. Substitution of nonfat milk for whole milk.

Reduction of cholesterol consumption to about 300 milligrams a day by decreasing consumption of butterfat, eggs, and other high cholesterol sources.

Reduction of sugar consumption by about 40 percent to account for about 15 percent of total calories.

Reduction of salt consumption by 50 to 85 percent, to approximately 3 grams a day.

First the cattle producers protested because of the recommendation to reduce the consumption of meat.

Then the sugar interests said the sugar recommendation had no scientific basis.

The National Canners Association was upset because the report suggested using fresh and frozen instead of canned vegetables.

The egg producers were upset and said cholesterol levels would not be lowered by reducing egg consumption.

The American Medical Association also weighed in and said the Goals should not be adopted because there is no proof that diet is related to disease. And, they added, changes in diet might lead to economic dislocation. The National Dairy Council endorsed the AMA's statement. Ironically, about the same time the AMA was attacking the report, the respected British medical journal *Lancet* praised it, saying, "The American goals will be welcomed by people who have thought seriously about the diet of Western man."

Those who wonder where the AMA was coming from would do well to remember that it was just about the last to admit that smoking is a cause of cancer. For years doctors endorsed cigarettes in ads.

The avalanche of industry pressure had its effect: some members of the Senate committee that had released the report vowed to disown the Goals if they were not modified. And so they were.

The revised Goals made their debut one year later, in January 1978, and included three reasonable changes, including two new recommendations:

Maintain ideal weight.
Use alcohol in moderation.

And it changed one goal to read:

Reduce sugar consumption by about 45 percent to account for 10 percent of caloric intake.

And then, instead of increasing carbohydrate consumption to account for 55 to 60 percent of caloric intake, the new goal read:

Increase consumption of complex carbohydrates and "naturally occurring" sugars from about 28 percent of caloric intake to about 48 percent.

About cholesterol, the modified Goals said that reducing cholesterol consumption does not mean elimination of egg consumption. Since eggs are only one source of dietary cholesterol, a specific recommendation as to the number of eggs necessary to meet the goal is inappropriate.

The recommendation to reduce salt consumption to about 3 grams a day was changed so that the suggested intake of salt was upped to 5 grams a day.

And finally, the recommendation to decrease consumption of meat and increase consumption of poultry and fish was changed to read:

> Decrease consumption of animal fat, and choose meats, poultry and fish which will reduce fat intake.

In the foreword to the revised Dietary Goals, Senator Robert Dole wrote: "I am pleased that the second edition deletes language from the first edition recommending 'eat less meat' and is not meant to recommend a reduction in intake of nutritious protein foods."

Three other senators, Charles Percy of Illinois, Richard Schweiker of Pennsylvania and Edward Zorinsky of Nebraska emphasized that they were not totally happy with the revised Goals because "the value of dietary change remains controversial and that science cannot at this time insure that an altered diet will provide improved protection from certain killer diseases such as heart disease and cancer."

They were protecting themselves from their food-industry constituents.

But even the modified Goals had champions in the Carter Administration's Department of Agriculture and Food and Drug Administration. They felt the government would be performing a valuable service to its constituents by making the Goals official government policy. This horrified the meat, dairy and egg producers, who shifted their lobbying efforts from Congress to USDA. Their success can be measured by comparing the specificity of even the second version of the Goals with the bland generalizations of the Guidelines that the government finally produced in February 1980.

Even though Dietary Guidelines for the United States offer no specifics on the amount of fat, sodium, complex carbohydrates, etc., that one should eat, the vast majority of nutritionists who believe that the recommendations are the most sensible we have follow the specifics for fat and cholesterol, complex carbohydrates and sodium found in the first version of Dietary Goals.

In the meantime, scores of other experts have come to essentially the same conclusions that originally prompted the Guidelines, and several important scientific organizations have endorsed them. Among the experts who believe similar dietary modifications are beneficial are the American Society for Clinical Nutrition, the former director of the National Cancer Institute, the Society for Nutrition Education, the American College of

Preventive Medicine and the Surgeon General. Even more compelling is the report released by the National Academy of Sciences in June 1982: "Diet, Nutrition and Cancer." It offers advice similar to, though more specific than, Dietary Guidelines on practices that may reduce the incidence of cancer. And at the end of 1983 the American Cancer Society endorsed those guidelines.

Despite this overwhelming support for the value of diet modification, segments of the food industry continued to try to undermine them. They worked through both the Reagan administration, which came to power in January 1981, and the Food and Nutrition Board of the National Research Council of the National Academy of Sciences. Among the members of the Food and Nutrition Board of the NAS are many scientists who earn substantial parts of their income from the food industry, as consultants, as spokespersons and as recipients of research grants. They include: Dr. Alfred E. Harper, who derives 10 percent of his income from positions as industry consultant to companies like Pillsbury and Kraft, the nation's largest cheese maker; Dr. Robert E. Olson, who is a research adviser and spokesperson for the American Egg Board and the Dairy Council of California. This work provides him with 10 percent of his income. In addition, Dr. David Kritchevsky has had a research grant from the egg industry, and Dr. Roslyn Alfin-Slater also has had an egg industry grant.

Two other members of the Food and Nutrition Board are Ogden Johnson, an executive with Hershey Foods, and Richard Hall, an executive with McCormick & Company.

The Food and Nutrition Board report, entitled "Toward More Healthful Diets" and released in 1981, contradicted the most controversial of the Guidelines' recommendations—those that suggest a reduction in fat and cholesterol intake. The report said healthy Americans do not need to reduce their intake of fat and cholesterol.

The report made the front pages of many newspapers across the country. But within a day or two, reporters started digging into the backgrounds of the members of the board that had prepared the document. Their disclosures cast a shadow on the validity of the findings, but still, its overall effect was to confuse Americans once again. Eventually, however, the importance of the report receded, and "Toward Healthful Diets" became just a footnote. Once again time caught up with the reactionaries: Within six months the highly respected *New England Journal of Medicine* reported the latest study linking a high-fat, high-cholesterol diet with increased risk of heart disease.

Meanwhile the anti-Guideline people had been busy on another front. And with the change in administration in 1981 they seized their opportunity to "get the government off their backs." It's what the new President had promised.

Reagan administration appointees replaced those who had been sympathetic to the idea of a federal government nutrition policy. The new appointees sided with industry. When Secretary of Agriculture John R. Block, a hog farmer, was asked at his Senate confirmation hearing how he felt about the government giving dietary advice to humans, he said, "I have to say people are pretty good at figuring out what to eat and what not to eat. I think people are going to balance their diets." Then he added that even a hog knows how to balance its ration. "A hog won't overeat," he said. "People surely are as smart as a hog. I'm not sure government should be into telling people what they should and shouldn't eat."

But Mr. Block found it wasn't so easy to clean house. Career civil servants, dietitians and nutritionists within USDA, who do not change when administrations change, disagreed with Mr. Block and the other political appointees like Richard Lyng, formerly director of the American Meat Institute, now deputy secretary of agriculture, and Bill (C. W.) McMillan, former president of the National Cattlemen's Association, now an assistant agriculture secretary. These civil servants felt that USDA should continue to supply the Dietary Guidelines brochure to the public free of charge and should continue research in human nutrition. They felt strongly that a booklet called "Food/2," designed to translate Dietary Guidelines into practical, usable menus, should be printed.

Their impact on Mr. Block was great enough that, in a speech in September 1981 to the American Dietetic Association, the secretary said "Food/2" would be printed and the Guidelines reissued. He said that the official government recommendations for sound eating would "remain the basis in our nutrition information and education programs" and would be reissued by the Government Printing Office.

The nutritionists in USDA were delighted. But their happiness was short-lived. As soon as Mr. Block made his speech, the phones started ringing off the hook at USDA. The beef, pork and egg producers and the American Farm Bureau were horrified, and they began to apply pressure.

So "Food/2" was recalled as it was on its way to the printer. Richard Lyng told me that it would be published "over my dead body." He said: "'Food/2' is all about how to lose weight and the question comes to mind very quickly, should government cutting school lunch and food stamps be spending money telling people how to diet?"

USDA turned publication of "Food/2" over to the American Dietetic Association, which agreed to break it into two parts, one part concerned with weight control, the other with fat and cholesterol. By doing so they suggest that only those with health problems have any interest in the part that deals with reduction of fat and cholesterol, while the part about weight control is for everyone. That, of course, defeats the purpose of the Guidelines, which are for healthy people.

For all intents and purposes USDA had gone out of the human nutrition advice business. But that apparently did not satisfy the critics of the Guidelines. In December 1982, USDA announced the formation of a panel to review the Guidelines and recommend "appropriate" changes. By this time you may even be able to guess the names of some of the panelists. If you said Dr. Robert E. Olson and Dr. David Kritchevsky, you would have been correct. In all, five of the nine scientists who were asked to join the panel have financial ties to the food industry; two of them were members of the Food and Nutrition Board that prepared the document "Toward More Healthful Diets."

Other members of the advisory panel include Dr. Edward Ahrens, who, at the request of the meat industry, testified against Dietary Goals when they were released; Dr. Frederick Stare, who has received retainers from the Cereal Institute, Kellogg and Nabisco to testify before Congress; and Dr. Bernard Schweigert, former assistant director of the American Meat Institute.

The Center for Science in the Public Interest, a Washington-based consumer group, filed comments before USDA protesting the makeup of the committee. They said the choice of panelists "is a clear sign that USDA does not intend to objectively review those dietary recommendations." CSPI said that if Secretary Block insists on tinkering with the Guidelines he should exclude anyone who has ties to the food industry and provide a "semblance of balance" by including members from health and citizens' groups. The results of the first committee meeting were predictable.

Dr. Olson said the cause-and-effect relationship between a high-fat diet and cardiovascular disease has not been established. He said the recommendation to avoid too much sugar "plays into the hands of food faddists."

By the second meeting, in December 1983, nothing had been resolved, though there appeared to be a general unwillingness to make wholesale changes in the Guidelines. Even segments of the beef and pork industries expressed general approval of the Guidelines as they are written, while the National Dairy Council suggested elimination of the fat, fiber and sugar guidelines. The recommendation about fat and cholesterol, however, continued to be the most controversial. But the January 1984 report from the National Institutes of Health on the benefits of lowering cholesterol levels may have finally quieted the critics. The report offers "the first conclusive evidence" that lowering blood cholesterol can prevent heart attacks. The advisory committee next meets after publication of this book. It will be interesting to see what they have to say in light of this latest evidence.

Meanwhile, in June 1982, the anti-Guidelines groups were struck another blow when the National Academy of Sciences released the aforementioned report entitled "Diet, Nutrition and Cancer." The report reinforces much of what the Dietary Guidelines recommend, but the new recommendations are made in an effort to reduce the risk of cancer. It differs from the Dietary Guidelines in a few significant ways:

The report does not find any evidence that saturated fat is more likely to cause cancer than unsaturated fat, and no recommendations are made about cholesterol.

Like the Guidelines, the cancer report encourages the consumption of fruits and vegetables but singles out those that contain vitamin C and beta-carotene, the precursor of vitamin A, because both nutrients appear to inhibit the formation of cancer.

The importance of specific vegetables, those from the cruciferous, or mustard, family—cabbage, broccoli, cauliflower, kale and brussels sprouts—is also stressed. Consumption of those vegetables, the report says, is associated with reduced incidence of stomach, colon and rectal cancer.

According to the report, data about the possible link between high protein intake and increased risk of cancer are insufficient to make a recommendation.

Evidence is also insufficient about the protective effects of fiber. However, the report emphasizes the importance of high-fiber, whole-grain cereal products.

The consumption of salt-cured (including salt-pickled) and smoked foods should be severely restricted, according to the report. And evidence about the roles of food additives and environmental contaminants is incomplete, though the report warns that collectively they may pose a risk.

The report calls the guidelines "interim," saying that "it is not now possible, and may never be possible, to specify a diet that would protect everyone against all forms of cancer. Nevertheless, the committee believes that it is possible, on the basis of current evidence, to formulate interim dietary guidelines that are both consistent with good nutritional practices and likely to reduce the risk of cancer."

Those who are opposed to modifications in the American diet are paddling upstream. But their greatest weapon in counteracting all the sound advice the scientists offer is still available to them, and that weapon is advertising. For as long as the industry continues to advertise junk food, Americans will continue to buy it. More and more people, however, are worrying about their diet and making efforts to improve it.

In a recent survey conducted by the restaurant industry and reported in the trade publication *Restaurants & Institutions:* "The healthy-foods fad has passed; it has become a broadly based, indelible pattern. For the young, 'lighter' foods promise slim figures; for the old, they combat poor health." Even as elegant and chic a restaurant as The Four Seasons in New York has added "Spa Cuisine" to its menu, featuring several appetizers and entrees that adhere to Dietary Guidelines.

Among the items most rapidly on the rise in restaurant orders are salads, fresh vegetables and fruits. Because critics of the dietary modifications recommended by both Dietary Guidelines and the "Diet, Nutrition and Cancer" report have not offered effective or practical alternatives, they have not been successful in subverting the advice. But until doctors and nutritionists all agree, changes in the food industry at both the manufacturing and farm levels will be slow to come. In the meantime, while

Americans may not follow the Guidelines as rigorously as they should, they know they exist, and some people are making an effort.

What people need to be convinced of now, more than anything else, is not that changes in eating habits are sensible but that the changes won't force them to eat food they don't like; that such food is not tasteless, boring, unappetizing, unattractive, unappealing, unsatisfying and meant for rabbits.

Well, it isn't. It's wonderful. The family menus in this book are based on the Dietary Guidelines and on the cancer report and they are just plain good to eat. They are so delicious that if you tell people that what they are eating is good *for* them, they may not believe you.

I was about to end this journey through the political thicket with that last sentence, but the December 4, 1983, issue of *Parade* magazine came to my attention, and it contains a story too important to ignore. Dietary Guidelines have a new ally—Ronald Reagan.

It may come as something of a shock to USDA, but President Reagan has endorsed the Guidelines. He obviously did not consult with his secretary of agriculture before he did so. In the article, which carried his byline, the President described his physical-fitness routine, one part of which dealt with eating. Of his eating habits he wrote, "The key here is moderation. I do watch what I eat.

"For example, at breakfast I pass up the pancakes and sausage in favor of cereal and fruit, skim milk and decaffeinated coffee. For lunch I have soup and a salad."

But on Thursdays at the White House Mess they have a Mexican lunch—tacos, enchiladas, beans and rice—and sometimes President Reagan indulges himself. "I tell myself I earned it," he wrote. "I cut down on the evening meal." The President's evening meals "usually consist of fish, chicken or meat with fresh vegetables and a salad of some kind.

"I eat moderately at the evening meal because I always hold a few calories back. I must confess I do like my desserts."

President Reagan also watches his salt intake. When he was governor of California a doctor told him he could live fifteen years longer if he broke the salt habit. "In less than a week," he wrote, "I cured myself of the salt habit."

Well, if that isn't Dietary Guidelines, I don't know what it is.

"DIETARY GOALS FOR THE UNITED STATES," JANUARY 1977

Increase complex carbohydrate consumption to account for 55 to 60 percent of caloric intake by increasing consumption of fruits, vegetables and whole grains.

Reduce overall fat consumption from approximately 40 percent to 30 percent by decreasing consumption of meat and increasing consumption of poultry and fish.

Reduce saturated fat consumption to account for about 10 percent of total calories; balanced with polyunsaturated and monounsaturated fats, which should account for about 10 percent of calories each. Substitute nonfat milk for whole milk.

Reduce cholesterol consumption to about 300 milligrams a day by decreasing consumption of butterfat, eggs and other high-cholesterol sources.

Reduce sugar consumption by about 40 percent to account for about 15 percent of total calories.

Reduce salt consumption by 50 to 85 percent to approximately 3 grams a day.

THE REVISED GOALS, JANUARY 1978

Maintain ideal weight.

Use alcohol in moderation.

Reduce sugar consumption by about 45 percent to account for 10 percent of caloric intake.

Increase consumption of complex carbohydrates and "naturally occurring" sugars from about 28 percent of caloric intake to about 48 percent.

"[Reducing cholesterol consumption] does not mean elimination of egg consumption. Since eggs are only one source of dietary cholesterol, a specific recommendation as to the number of eggs necessary to meet the goal is inappropriate."

Reduce salt consumption to 5 grams a day.

Decrease consumption of animal fat, and choose meats, poultry and fish which will reduce fat intake.

"DIETARY GUIDELINES FOR THE UNITED STATES," FEBRUARY 1980

Eat a variety of foods.

Maintain ideal weight.

Avoid too much fat, saturated fat, and cholesterol.

Eat foods with adequate starch and fiber.

Avoid too much sugar.

Avoid too much sodium.

If you drink alcohol, do so in moderation.

GUIDELINES BASED ON "DIETARY GUIDELINES" AND THE NATIONAL ACADEMY OF SCIENCES' REPORT, "DIET, NUTRITION AND CANCER," JUNE 1982

As a general rule, each day you should eat six or more servings of fruits and vegetables; five servings of whole grains; two or three servings of protein-rich foods. Accessory foods, such as fats and sweets, should be eaten in moderation.

Fruits and vegetables: A serving is ½ cup raw, cooked or frozen fruits or vegetables, or one piece of fresh fruit. Fresh or frozen fruits and vegetables are preferable to canned.

☐ Fruits and vegetables high in vitamins C or A are: strawberries, citrus fruits, cantaloupe, watermelon, mango, papaya, broccoli, butternut squash, brussels sprouts, cabbage, acorn squash, spinach, kale, escarole, romaine lettuce, parsley, red and green peppers, white potatoes, sweet potatoes, carrots.

Whole grains and cereals: One serving is one slice of bread, one small muffin or ½ cup cooked cereal.

☐ Foods you can think of as "whole grain" include brown rice, corn and cornmeal, wheat germ, bran, barley, buckwheat flour and groats, bulgur wheat, oatmeal and whole-wheat flour, bread and crackers.

☐ Whole grains are preferable to enriched, refined grains because they are important sources of thiamin, riboflavin and iron; they also supply fiber, vitamin B_6, magnesium and zinc.

Protein-rich foods: A serving is one cup skim milk, 1½ ounces hard cheese, one cup low-fat yogurt, 2 or 3 ounces boneless fish, meat or poultry or one egg; one cup cooked beans; or ¼ cup nuts.

☐ Dairy products should be low-fat. High-fat dairy foods include whole-milk products, cream, most cheeses, ice cream and sour cream.

☐ Dairy products contain calcium, riboflavin, protein, vitamins A and B_{12}. Foods that have been fortified will supply vitamin D.

☐ To reduce fat content of meats, trim off exterior fat; choose meat with little marbling; eat white-meat poultry and remove skin.

☐ Meat and poultry are valuable sources of protein, phosphorus, vitamins B_6 and B_{12}, iron and zinc.

☐ If you are watching your cholesterol intake, limit your consumption of eggs and organ meats.

☐ Dried beans include lentils, chickpeas (garbanzos) and dried peas.

☐ Nuts are high in fat.

Accessory foods: Fats, sweets, alcohol, sodium.

☐ In addition to oil, butter and margarine, foods high in fat include mayonnaise, salad dressings, rich desserts, fried and creamed foods and processed meats such as liverwurst, frankfurters and bologna.

☐ Animal fats are higher in saturated fats than most vegetable oils (except coconut and palm oils). Read labels.

☐ There is no nutritional value other than calories in alcohol or sugar. Brown sugar and honey are no more nutritious than white sugar.

☐ Reduce sodium consumption by limiting intake of salty snacks such as potato chips, pretzels, crackers and pickles. Limit intake of soy sauce, Worcestershire sauce, catsup, mustard, some meat tenderizers, monosodium glutamate, gravy mixes, canned soups, processed meats such as bacon, frankfurters and bologna.

☐ Restrict intake of salt-cured, smoked and nitrite-cured foods.

☐ Check labels of canned products. Some now list sodium content.

Family Meals

Frozen main-dish menus;
30-minute family menus

NOTE: In the list below, F indicates that the dish may be prepared ahead of time and frozen.

SUMMER MENU FOR 3   40

Honey ginger chicken (F)
Chinese vermicelli
Tomatoes and onions in vermouth

ALL SEASONS MENU FOR 4   42

Chicken with Indian spices (F)
Brown rice
Cucumbers in mustard-yogurt sauce

FALL MENU FOR 4   44

Chicken with apples and ginger (F)
Noodles
Red peppers and onions

SUMMER–FALL MENU FOR 4   46

Chicken breasts with ratatouille (F)
Macaroni shells

SUMMER MENU FOR 3   48

Chicken with cumin-cinnamon marinade (F)
New potatoes with dill
Sesame broccoli
Fresh peaches with orange liqueur

ALL SEASONS MENU FOR 4   50

Chicken Provençal and macaroni (F)
Melon wedge

FALL—WINTER MENU FOR 3 74

Ground turkey balls (F)
Zucchini sautéed with fennel
Herbed barley
Fruit Ice

SUMMER MENU FOR 4 76

Picadillo (F)
Toasted tortillas
Maquechou

SUMMER MENU FOR 3 78

Athenian-style ground meat with tomatoes and scallions (F)

ALL SEASONS MENU FOR 4 80

Vegetarian lasagna (F)
Red pepper salad

ALL SEASONS MENU FOR 3 82

Fragrant brown rice (F)
Radish and cheese salad
Spiced zucchini

ALL SEASONS MENU FOR 3 84

Broiled eggplant, cheese and tomato sauce (F)
Green noodles
Greens with buttermilk dressing

FALL—WINTER MENU FOR 4 86

Kasha, corn and cheese casserole (F)
Apple-walnut salad with chutney-yogurt dressing

ALL SEASONS MENU FOR 4 88

Tomato sauce Provençal (F)
Pasta
Spinach-almond salad

"It's sensible to be thinking about nutrition," says Julia Child, America's foremost interpreter of French cooking. "The French enhance flavors by reductions, wine and herbs. And fresh foods are extremely important," she adds.

Mrs. Child's sentiments are echoed by many of her culinary peers. Giuliano Bugialli, cookbook author and master teacher, describing Italian dishes as the food of the '80s, says, "Italians eat a lot of vegetables; and since we don't destroy them, we get all the vitamins."

Though they probably don't know it, Mrs. Child and Mr. Bugialli are expounding the basic tenets of that controversial document, "Dietary Guidelines for the United States" and a more recent scientific publication from the National Academy of Sciences, "Diet, Nutrition and Cancer." Neither can be described as a treatise on haute cuisine, but our best cooks are saying what the government is saying—good food and good nutrition can be synonymous.

The forty-five menus in this chapter are based on both these reports and on the principles of good cooking. Flavor is as important as the nutritional value in each of them. They provide exciting new tastes and complexities of seasoning that are far more delicious and satisfying than the simpleminded convenience foods in which the predominant, and sometimes only, seasoning is salt. Included in each of the menus is the most essential nutrition information: calorie count, percentage of fat, milligrams of sodium and grams of fiber—the basics you need to determine what to eat the rest of the day and still stay within the limits of the nutrition guidelines.

I have created meals that are low in calories on the theory that it's much easier and healthier to increase the caloric content by adding more bread, rice or noodles or dessert. The menus are also low in sodium because salt is not used in the preparation. For those who must have it, salt is easy to add at the table. All but seven of the menus contain 35 percent fat or less, and thirty-two of them contain 30 percent fat or less. Most nutrition experts now believe that a diet deriving 30 percent of its calories from fat is the most desirable, so when you choose a dinner that provides more than 30 percent, you can adjust the other meals accordingly. Those are the days to eat fruit and vegetable salads with low-fat dressings, vegetable soups, cereals, toast or

English muffins with jelly but no butter, to order low-fat fish broiled without butter or white-meat chicken without skin. All the meals are also high in fiber, featuring more vegetables and whole-grain products than usually found in American meals. Eating a lot of fiber is a wonderful way to reduce the number of calories you need to make you feel full.

These meals are no more difficult to make from scratch than the traditional American diet in which three quarters of a pound of meat or more forms the basis of the meal. They lend themselves to speedy last-minute preparation as well as cooking ahead and freezing. The menus have been divided into two categories: those with frozen, prepare-ahead main dishes that leave last-minute cooking to one or two side dishes—actual preparation time before dinner often taking no more than ten minutes (these are marked with an F)—plus a brand-new collection of thirty-minute meals, a contribution from my last book, *Keep It Simple*—the entire meal is prepared in just thirty minutes and eaten as soon as it is ready.

The menus featuring frozen main dishes are in response to a large segment of working people who like to do things ahead, who cook on weekends, often with help from another person. With the shopping done, it should take one person no more than four hours to make five main dishes. There are six weeks (or thirty) of these weekday menus with main dishes that are cooked, then frozen in portions suitable for the family's use. Some of the menus are for two, some for four. Any of them can be doubled easily so that cooks can, if they like, prepare one main dish to use twice in the same week, cutting down considerably on the advance work.

Ingredients not needed until the dish is defrosted and ready to be cooked and served are separated from the other ingredients by a space.

Included with each frozen main-dish menu is a game plan for putting the meal together before dinner. The game plans are there at the request of a fan of the previous book. Just as I was finishing this book, I received a call from a bachelor father, as he described himself, who lives in Vermont. He was calling just to tell me that *Keep It Simple* had kept him from "going nuts." And the thing he liked best about it was the game plan that accompanied each menu.

Here are some suggestions to make the work go more smoothly.

To cut down on preparation time before dinner, if possible the main course should be defrosted the night before. If there is substantial density and volume to the dish, it can be safely placed on the kitchen counter to defrost overnight, unless the kitchen is especially warm. In that case, or if the volume of the dish is very small, it should be defrosted overnight in the refrigerator, taken out in the morning to defrost a little more before you go to work and returned to the refrigerator until you come home. You will have to make that judgment, taking into account the bulk of the food and the temperature in your kitchen. If you forget to defrost a meal, all is not lost; it can be heated very slowly from the frozen stage at dinnertime.

Proper wrapping for storage is important to preserve the flavor of those frozen dishes. If paper is used it should be nonporous. Overwrapping with plastic bags is easy and helpful. Plastic containers should have tight-fitting lids.

Anything frozen should be marked carefully, and that is why I have included the stickers in the book. Have you ever tried to figure out what that unmarked mystery package contained just a week after you put it in the freezer? Because it's difficult to write on many containers, a fact I discovered when I was writing this book, these stickers are designed to take care of the problem. Each has space for the name of the dish, the number of people it serves and the date it was frozen.

Short-term storage in a freezer that is contained inside the refrigerator door is all right. But for storing longer than a week, it is best to have a freezer that has a separate door. It isn't that the frozen foods stored at more than 0 degrees are unsafe to eat, but they lose some of their quality and develop "off" flavors from the constant opening and closing of the door, which raises and lowers the temperature in the freezer.

If by chance you should find yourself with any of these main dishes in the freezer after several months, don't worry. We have been eating some that I had frozen six months ago and they were excellent.

Because the response to *Keep It Simple* was so overwhelming, I also decided to offer three weeks of new menus that are completed in thirty minutes—that is, from the time the groceries are taken out of the cupboard or the shopping bag until the meal is ready to be put on the table. This assumes that whoever is *not* doing the cooking is at least capable of setting the table, and that includes all able-bodied men and women over the age of five.

To prepare these menus in thirty minutes you will have to concentrate on the preparation of the meal. Talking on the phone, feeding the baby, sitting down to read the mail all interfere with the game plan and add to your preparation time. Cooking the meal requires undivided attention, but only for thirty minutes.

You need to know where things are in the kitchen, the knives have to be sharp, the breakfast dishes already washed or at least in the dishwasher.

You cannot be a stickler for measurements; cooks who know their way around the kitchen can tell by looking. If you have a food processor—and so many people do these days that I have used it in some recipes—you can speed up the cooking time for many dishes, especially if you want to make large quantities. I have not, however, found that I saved much time if I used the processor for chopping one onion: It takes much longer to wash four parts of the appliance than one knife.

A toaster oven is another nice kitchen amenity for a small family. Not only is it quicker than an oven, it costs much less to operate. If you are in the market for one, buy the model in which you can broil foods, too.

Be sure to read the recipes before starting and use the game plan as a guide. But remember it is just a guide. You will sometimes find it necessary to move steps around.

There is also a shopping list for the foods you are not likely to have in the house as staples. The lists may include foods you would not ordinarily consider staples. Sometimes I call foods staples even when they are not used often because they will last for months and require trips to special markets to buy. If I have them on hand, it's one less trip to make just before dinner. See page 38 for my suggested list of staples and other ingredients that would be nice to have on hand but are not essential.

The shopping list gives the amount needed of an ingredient in parentheses if it is less than or different from the way it is sold at the store. Example: Bunch parsley (2 tablespoons).

All of the menus are designed for busy people. Yet they use only minimally processed foods. With the exception of canned tomato products, a can of beans and frozen peas, no canned or frozen products are called for. Not just because prepared foods often contain undesirable additives, but because they hardly ever taste as good as fresh.

The greatest challenge in putting these menus together was reducing the fat. I had to do a considerable amount of juggling and reworking of the dishes. With the help of Linda Smith, a registered dietitian in Washington, who did the nutrient analysis, I was aiming for 30 to 35 percent calories from fat. Controlling sodium* and calories and adding enough fiber were relatively simple. This is an example of how old recipes were revised to meet new standards of nutrition without destroying good taste standards.

"Old style" meat sauce   (4 SERVINGS)

2 tablespoons vegetable oil	1 6-ounce can tomato paste
1 pound ground beef	1 8-ounce can tomato sauce
1 green pepper, chopped	2 teaspoons salt
2 small onions, chopped	3 teaspoons sugar
2 garlic cloves, minced	1 teaspoon dried oregano leaves
1 16-ounce can tomatoes	

Heat the oil and brown the meat. Add the pepper, onions and garlic and sauté for five minutes. Add the remaining ingredients; stir, simmer covered for 1½ to 2 hours.

* Sodium range for recipes is approximately 50 milligrams, depending on where you live.

MENU ANALYSIS SUMMARY

	NUTRIENTS PER SERVING		
	CALORIES	% FAT	SODIUM (MG)*
"Old style" meat sauce	625	85	2,186

* MG = milligrams

"Nouvelle" meat sauce†   (4 SERVINGS)

2 tablespoons vegetable oil

1 pound ground turkey

1 large onion, chopped

2 cloves garlic, minced or put through press

3 large tomatoes, coarsely chopped

6-ounce can no-salt-added tomato paste

2 tablespoons chopped fresh oregano or 2 teaspoons dried oregano leaves

1 tablespoon chopped fresh basil or 1 teaspoon dried basil

1 cup dry red wine

Freshly ground black pepper to taste

Heat 1 tablespoon oil and sauté turkey in it until pink color is gone, stirring to break up pieces. Set turkey to one side in pan. Add remaining oil and sauté onion and garlic in it until onion is limp.

Stir in tomatoes, tomato paste, oregano, basil, red wine and pepper. Simmer one hour, until mixture thickens.

MENU ANALYSIS SUMMARY

	NUTRIENTS PER SERVING		
	CALORIES	% FAT	SODIUM (MG)
"Nouvelle" meat sauce	500	31	94

In order to revise the traditional recipes to fit the new way of eating, these are some of the special techniques I used and recommend to you:

Buy no-salt-added tomato products; low-fat (1 or 2 percent) dairy products and when possible no-salt-added dairy products such as cottage cheese and sweet butter; reduced-sodium soy sauce; brown rice; whole-grain breads; fresh, in-season fruits and vegetables.

Use plain, low-fat yogurt in place of sour cream. To keep yogurt from

† (This recipe is part of the menu on page 70.)

separating when it is heated, add cornstarch, mixing one tablespoon of cornstarch with one cup of yogurt before cooking.

Use corn oil when vegetable oil is indicated. Olive oil is also good because it is neither saturated nor unsaturated fat; it is monosaturated.

Do not use salt. Cook instead with lemon juice, vinegar, hot pepper sauce, herbs and spices.

Standard salad dressing recipes call for a three-to-one oil-to-vinegar or -lemon-juice ratio. Not only is it unnecessary, it makes the salad taste oily. Reduce the ratio to equal parts oil and acid or use half again as much oil as acid. The ratio depends on the kind of vinegar you use and the other dressing ingredients. I find that balsamic vinegar, a delicious, very mild Italian vinegar, needs very little oil to produce a tasty dressing. Start with less oil; you can always add more, but you can't remove it.

Use one tablespoon of dressing per serving of salad. It is more than enough if you toss the salad well. Always remember that low-calorie foods, like salads, need very little fat to make the fat percentage soar. Take a look at the percentage of fat in the salad components of the menus to see how that applies.

Use less oil to brown foods. One tablespoon is enough for several onions or for half a chicken, yet three or four times those amounts are often called for.

Trim all exterior fat from meats and pour off all fat that accumulates in the pan after cooking. The fat has already made its contribution to the flavor of the dish.

Remove the skin from chicken and then brown meat carefully. Skinless chicken, properly browned, is crisp without being dry.

Use ground turkey in place of ground beef in sauces, meat loaves and meatballs.

Steam, poach, broil, bake and boil instead of fry or sauté. Try poaching chicken or fish in vermouth. Cook onions in stock or vermouth.

Substitute some egg whites for whole eggs.

Limit the amount of cheese as well as the amount of meat; most cheeses are very high in fat and sodium.

Steam vegetables in place of boiling to retain more nutrients and to produce a prettier-looking vegetable.

Don't peel vegetables such as potatoes, carrots and cucumbers unless it is necessary. If you must peel, do so after cooking and you will lose fewer nutrients.

Don't throw away the outer leaves of the lettuce unless they are rusty. The outer leaves contain more calcium, iron and vitamin A.

Cook the leaves with the broccoli; they, too, are rich in nutrients.

Help your body absorb more iron from iron-rich foods by combining them with citrus: lemon juice with spinach, orange juice with poultry.

The one concession I cannot make is to substitute margarine for butter.

So little is used in these menus it will contribute minimal amounts of cholesterol to the diet and there is no comparison in taste.

A few of the menus recommend dessert and then usually fruit or fruit ice, not sherbet, which contains milk. They help to lower the percentage of fat in the meal while increasing the calories. A slice or two of bread will accomplish the same purpose. There are enough menus in the chapter that are so low in calories they could easily be part of an overall diet plan.

For those who need more calories in menus where they are low, add bread and desserts or simply increase the amount of the dishes that are not high in fat.

When you work with these basic principles you will learn to create meals and to develop many of your own menus—all of which follow the latest dietary guidelines.

Staples for **You've Got It Made** kitchen

SPICES

Allspice

Anise

Basil

Bay leaves

Caraway seeds

Cardamom, ground

Cayenne

Celery seeds

Chile powder, mild

Cinnamon

Cloves

Coriander seeds, ground

Cumin seeds, ground

Curry powder

Dillweed

Fennel seeds

Ginger, fresh and powdered*

Marjoram leaves

Mustard, dried powder

Nutmeg, ground

Oregano leaves

Paprika, Hungarian sweet

Pepper, freshly ground black and white

Rosemary

Savory

Tarragon

Thyme leaves

Turmeric

* Keep fresh ginger in freezer and grate off as needed

CONDIMENTS

Reduced-sodium soy sauce

Tamari (nice but not essential)

Oriental sesame paste†

Chunky peanut butter (nice but not essential)

Lemons

Capers

Dijon mustard

Worcestershire sauce

Black olives packed in brine, French or Greek (nice but not essential)

† Oriental sesame paste is made with toasted sesame seeds; Middle Eastern is made with untoasted. The toasted has a deeper flavor.

Honey

No-salt-added tomato paste, puree and whole tomatoes

Dried black mushrooms (nice but not essential)

Sesame seeds (nice but not essential)

Raisins (nice but not essential)

Apple juice (nice but not essential)

Canned green chiles (nice but not essential)

Cheeses (nice but not essential): Parmesan, sharp such as cheddar

Oils: corn, sesame, olive plus the following which are nice but not essential: hot sesame also called hot chili, peanut, hazelnut or walnut

Vinegars: white, rice, tarragon, white wine and red wine, preferably balsamic

PASTAS AND GRAINS (nice but not essential)

Lasagna
Linguine
Spaghetti
Rotini
Spiral
Tubular

Angel hair
Medium and thin egg noodles
Cellophane
Green noodles
Bulgur

BASICS

Garlic
Brown rice
Unsalted butter
Cornstarch
Flour

Eggs
Milk
No-salt-added broth or stock: beef, chicken and vegetable
Yogurt, plain, low-fat

Honey ginger chicken (F)
Chinese vermicelli
Tomatoes and onions in vermouth

If you've been craving a hot fudge sundae or a piece of pecan pie, this is the meal at which to have it!

MENU ANALYSIS SUMMARY

	NUTRIENTS PER SERVING		
	CALORIES	% FAT	SODIUM (MG)*
Honey ginger chicken	140	19	283
Chinese vermicelli	210	0	2
Tomatoes and onions in vermouth	84	11	13
Totals for each individual/meal	434	10	298

Fiber per person: about 4 grams

* MG = milligrams

GAME PLAN

Turn oven to 500 degrees.

Boil water for vermicelli.

Prepare onions and tomatoes.

Roast chicken.

Sauté onions.

Soak vermicelli.

Turn chicken two or three times.

Drain vermicelli.

Add tomatoes and savory to onions. Season.

Broil chicken.

Honey ginger chicken (F)   (3 SERVINGS)

- 1 chicken breast, 2 drumsticks and 2 thighs, skinned
- 4 tablespoons finely chopped onion
- 1½ tablespoons honey
- 1 tablespoon reduced-sodium soy sauce
- 1 tablespoon minced or grated fresh ginger
- 2 medium cloves garlic, minced
- 2 tablespoons sherry
- ¼ cup thinly sliced scallions

Cut the breast in half and remove breastbone. Combine the onion, honey, soy sauce, ginger, garlic and sherry. Arrange chicken pieces in single layer, preferably in baking dish that can go into the oven as well as the freezer. Spoon the marinade mixture evenly over chicken pieces. Wrap for freezer and freeze.

To serve, return to room temperature and bake at 500 degrees for about 27 minutes. Turn once or twice. Run baking dish under broiler to brown, if necessary, but watch carefully or the chicken will burn and dry out. Remove chicken. Deglaze pan with three tablespoons water.

Serve with juices from bottom of the pan, which are especially good over the Chinese vermicelli.

Sprinkle with scallions.

Chinese vermicelli   (3 SERVINGS)

6 ounces Chinese vermicelli

Bring hot water to boil in kettle. Pour over vermicelli and allow to soak about 15 minutes. Drain thoroughly.

Serve with some of sauce from chicken.

Tomatoes and onions in vermouth   (3 SERVINGS)

½ pound onions, chopped
3 tablespoons dry vermouth
3 medium ripe tomatoes
1½ teaspoons dried savory
Freshly ground black pepper
to taste

Sauté the onions in hot vermouth in skillet for about 7 to 10 minutes, until vermouth has evaporated and onions soften and begin to color.

Chop tomatoes into large chunks. Add to onions with savory, which is crumbled between your fingers as it is sprinkled on the tomatoes. Mix and season with pepper. Cook about 3 minutes, stirring occasionally, and serve.

Chicken with Indian spices (F)
Brown rice
Cucumbers in mustard-yogurt sauce

This is a low-fat, low-sodium meal. You could add a rich dessert if you like, or some whole-grain bread. It's a good meal for a day when you have had a big, rich lunch or breakfast.

MENU ANALYSIS SUMMARY

	NUTRIENTS PER SERVING		
	CALORIES	% FAT	SODIUM (MG)
Chicken with Indian spices	281	32	126
Brown rice	176	5	4
Cucumbers in mustard-yogurt sauce	35	26	24
Totals for each individual/meal	492	22	154

Fiber per person: about 8 grams

GAME PLAN

Cook rice.

Heat chicken.

Prepare cucumber salad.

Chicken with Indian spices (F) (4 SERVINGS)

1 teaspoon turmeric

1 teaspoon ground cumin powder

1 teaspoon ground coriander

½ teaspoon ground ginger

⅛ teaspoon pure chile powder*
Freshly ground black pepper to taste

3 tablespoons unsalted butter

4 large skinless and boneless chicken breast halves, cubed

2 large onions, finely chopped

2 large tomatoes, cut in small chunks

2 large green peppers, finely chopped

1 stalk celery, finely chopped

4 sprigs fresh parsley, minced

1 large clove garlic, minced or put through press

⅓ cup raisins

1 tablespoon dry sherry

1½ teaspoons lemon juice

* Chile powder contains only chile, the pepper. There are no other spices in it. It comes in various strengths from mild to fiery hot. Choose the one to suit your taste.

Brown spices over high heat in 2 tablespoons butter for 1 minute. Add chicken, stir to coat and brown 1 more minute. Set chicken aside.

Add remaining butter to pan; heat and sauté onions over high heat until limp. Add remaining vegetables, garlic, chicken, raisins, sherry and lemon juice and cook over medium heat until vegetables give off juices and celery is tender but slightly crisp.

Freeze in portions suitable for your family's needs.

To serve, defrost; heat through and serve over rice.

Brown rice   (4 SERVINGS)

1 cup brown rice   2 cups water

The night before, or no less than 2 hours before serving, cover the rice with the water and allow to sit in cooking pot.

To serve, bring water and rice to boil; reduce heat and simmer rice in covered pot until tender and water has been absorbed, 17 to 20 minutes.

Cucumbers in mustard-yogurt sauce   (4 SERVINGS)

½ cup plain, low-fat yogurt
1½ teaspoons Dijon-style mustard
3 dashes hot pepper sauce or to taste

¾ pound Kirby cucumbers or regular cucumbers

In serving bowl mix yogurt with mustard and hot pepper sauce.

If using Kirby cucumbers, scrub, do not peel, and slice thinly. If using regular waxed cucumbers, peel and then slice.

Mix cucumbers with dressing and chill until serving time.

Chicken with apples and ginger (F)
Noodles
Red peppers and onions

This meal can be on the table in 20 minutes—only taking as long to prepare as it takes for the chicken to cook.

MENU ANALYSIS SUMMARY

	NUTRIENTS PER SERVING		
	CALORIES	% FAT	SODIUM (MG)
Chicken with apples and ginger	607	36	270
Noodles	236	0	2
Red peppers and onions	73	74	21
Totals for each individual/meal	916	32	293

Fiber per person: 9 grams

GAME PLAN

Boil water in covered pot for noodles.

Prepare peppers and onions and sauté.

Heat chicken.

Cook noodles.

Season peppers and onions.

Chicken with apples and ginger (F) (4 SERVINGS)

3-pound chicken, cut into 16 pieces

2 tablespoons corn oil

1 large onion, chopped

1 clove garlic, minced

¼ cup dry white wine

1 cup apple juice

1 tablespoon finely chopped fresh ginger

1 cup plain, low-fat yogurt

1 tablespoon cornstarch

2 well-flavored apples, cored and cut into small chunks

Freshly ground black pepper to taste

8 ounces medium egg noodles (2 ounces per person)

Remove as much skin and external fat as possible from chicken. Heat oil in skillet large enough to hold chicken pieces in single layer. Brown chicken on both sides in hot oil over medium heat. Remove and set aside.

Sauté onion and garlic in same pan until onion is soft. Add to pan wine, apple juice and ginger and cook over medium-high heat until liquid is reduced to 1 cup.

Stir cornstarch into yogurt. Add to pan with apples and chicken and season with pepper.

Freeze. To serve, defrost and cook on top of stove, covered, for 20 minutes or until heated through thoroughly.

While chicken cooks, cook noodles.

Red peppers and onions (4 SERVINGS)

4 large red peppers, thinly sliced

3 large onions, thinly sliced

1½ tablespoons olive oil

2 tablespoons red wine vinegar

Freshly ground black pepper to taste

Sauté the peppers and onions in hot oil about 10 minutes, until onions and peppers are softened. Season with vinegar and pepper and serve.

Chicken breasts with ratatouille (F)
Macaroni shells

A very low-fat meal. Would be ideal to plan to have this on a day you know you are likely to have a higher-fat lunch (hamburger, for example) or a rich brunch. You could also add a nice pastry dessert to this meal and be within 35 percent fat.

MENU ANALYSIS SUMMARY

	NUTRIENTS PER SERVING		
	CALORIES	% FAT	SODIUM (MG)
Chicken breasts	252	39	329
Ratatouille	110	8	83
Macaroni shells	319	0	3
Totals for each individual/meal	681	17	415

Fiber per person: about 7 grams

GAME PLAN

Bring water to boil for macaroni in covered pot.

Cook chicken.

Cook macaroni.

Chicken breasts with ratatouille (F)　　　(4 SERVINGS)

4 large chicken breast halves, skinned and boned

Freshly ground black pepper to taste

2 tablespoons corn oil

4 cups Ratatouille Base (see recipe next page)

4 tablespoons coarsely grated Parmesan cheese

12 ounces macaroni shells

Sprinkle chicken breasts with pepper. Sauté in hot oil over medium-high heat until browned on both sides.

Spread half of the ratatouille on bottom of shallow baking dish; top with chicken breasts; top breasts with remaining ratatouille, making sure they are well covered. Sprinkle with cheese.

Freeze. To serve, defrost and cook in covered pan on top of stove over medium-low heat for 20 to 25 minutes.

Meanwhile, cook macaroni. If desired, run chicken under broiler to brown cheese.

Ratatouille base

2½ pounds eggplant, cut into 1-inch cubes

7 sprigs fresh dill

2½ pounds zucchini, cut into ¼-inch-thick slices

1¼ pounds onions, sliced

3 green peppers, cut into 1-inch pieces

2 large or 3 medium cloves garlic, put through garlic press

6 sprigs fresh parsley

1 teaspoon dried oregano

1 pound fresh plum tomatoes or 1-pound can no-salt-added plum tomatoes

3 tablespoons drained capers

6 to 8 tablespoons white vinegar
Freshly ground black pepper to taste

Do not peel eggplant. Remove tough stems from dill. Place all ingredients in one large or two smaller pots. Mix contents of pot to coat and distribute seasonings.

Cover and cook over low heat, just below simmer, for 45 minutes. When vegetables are soft, ratatouille is cooked. Drain well.

Divide in half. Use one half for Chicken Breasts with Ratatouille; use the remaining half for fish (see recipe page 104).

Chicken with cumin-cinnamon marinade (F)
New potatoes with dill
Sesame broccoli
Fresh peaches with orange liqueur

If you want to serve this meal when peaches are out of season, use an orange or tangelo instead.

MENU ANALYSIS SUMMARY

	NUTRIENTS PER SERVING		
	CALORIES	% FAT	SODIUM (MG)
Chicken with cumin-cinnamon marinade	289	65	72
New potatoes with dill	93	0	8
Sesame broccoli	106	51	35
1 whole-grain roll	125	0	117
1 Large fresh peach with 1 ounce orange liqueur	175	0	0
Totals for each individual/meal	788	31	232

Fiber per person: 8 grams

GAME PLAN

Slice peaches and pour a little liqueur over them.

Prepare and cook potatoes.

Heat oil for chicken.

Remove chicken from marinade and brown chicken.

Prepare broccoli.

Boil water for broccoli.

Turn chicken thighs.

Prepare dressing for broccoli.

Add onion marinade to chicken; cover and cook.

Mince dill.

Cook broccoli.

Turn chicken.

Quarter potatoes; season with pepper and dill.

Mix broccoli with dressing; sprinkle with pepper and sesame seeds.

Chicken with cumin-cinnamon marinade (F)   (3 SERVINGS)

2 medium cloves garlic
⅓ cup finely chopped onion
½ cup dry red wine
2 tablespoons olive oil
1 teaspoon ground cumin

½ teaspoon ground cinnamon
Freshly ground black pepper to taste
6 chicken thighs, skin removed
1½ tablespoons corn oil

Chop garlic in food processor by turning on food processor and putting each clove through top while blade is whirling. Turn off machine and add chopped onion, wine, olive oil, cumin, cinnamon and pepper.

Process until mixture is a paste.

Place thighs in a single layer in a container suitable for the freezer. Distribute the onion mixture evenly over the top of each thigh. Freeze.

To serve, defrost as many thighs as you need. Then scrape off marinade, reserving.

Heat corn oil in skillet. Brown thighs on both sides, starting with the side that was coated with the marinade.

Reduce heat and spread reserved onion marinade on both sides of each thigh; cover and simmer about 15 minutes, turning once, until chops are done.

NOTE TO COOK: Scrapings from pot are good over potatoes.

New potatoes with dill   (3 SERVINGS)

1 pound tiny new potatoes
Freshly ground black pepper
to taste

3 tablespoons minced fresh dill

Scrub potatoes but do not peel.

Cook in water to cover in covered pot until tender, about 20 minutes. Drain; do not peel.

Place in serving bowl; cut in quarters or halves; sprinkle with pepper and dill.

Sesame broccoli   (3 SERVINGS)

1½ pounds broccoli
1 teaspoon Oriental sesame oil
1 teaspoon rice vinegar

1½ teaspoons sesame seeds
Freshly ground black pepper
to taste

Remove tough stems from broccoli, wash and cut heads into florets. Steam for about 7 minutes, until broccoli is tender but still crisp.

Meanwhile, in serving dish mix the oil with the vinegar. Add the broccoli and mix gently to coat. Sprinkle with sesame seeds and pepper.

Chicken Provençal and macaroni (F)
Melon wedge

The meal is fairly high in sodium because of the olives. It's a good day to have cereal for breakfast, fruit salad, broiled fish or chicken for lunch.

MENU ANALYSIS SUMMARY

	NUTRIENTS PER SERVING		
	CALORIES	% FAT	SODIUM (MG)
Chicken Provençal and macaroni	474	37	737
½ small melon	60	0	2
Totals for each individual/meal	534	31	739

Fiber per person: 6½ grams

GAME PLAN

Bring water to boil in covered pot for macaroni.

Prepare zucchini and add to chicken.

Cook chicken with zucchini.

Cook macaroni.

Prepare melon.

1 medium onion, chopped
1 medium clove garlic, minced or put through press
2½ tablespoons olive oil
17-ounce can no-salt-added Italian tomatoes
1 teaspoon dried oregano
1 teaspoon dried thyme
1 bay leaf

½ teaspoon dried rosemary
Freshly ground black pepper to taste
3- to 3½-pound chicken
½ cup dry white wine
½ cup pitted black olives, packed in brine

3 medium zucchini
12 ounces large tubular macaroni

Sauté onion and garlic in 1½ teaspoons hot oil until onion is soft. Add tomatoes, breaking up pieces with your fingers, along with juice from can. Add oregano, thyme, bay leaf, rosemary and black pepper to taste. Cook over low heat, 20 minutes, stirring occasionally.

Meanwhile, cut up chicken, removing first two joints of chicken wings and saving for soup. Skin remaining chicken. Sauté in 2 tablespoons hot olive oil about 5 minutes on each side, turning once and allowing to brown.

Add tomato sauce, wine and olives; mix well and freeze.

To serve, defrost. Scrub zucchini and cut into ½-inch-thick slices. Add zucchini to chicken.

Cover and cook chicken for 15 to 20 minutes over low heat, until chicken is tender and zucchini is done but not mushy.

Meanwhile cook the macaroni in boiling water until tender but not soft.

Spoon macaroni on individual plates and arrange chicken and sauce over it.

Sichuan peanut sauce with fish or chicken (F)
Stir-fried peppers and onions
Brown rice

If you add an additional ¼ cup raw rice (steamed) per person, total calories will be 614; it changes percentage of fat in meal to 28.

The fat content increases a little if you use skinless chicken thighs.

MENU ANALYSIS SUMMARY

	NUTRIENTS PER SERVING		
	CALORIES	% FAT	SODIUM (MG)
Sichuan peanut sauce	105	71	99
With fish or chicken	166	11	115
Stir-fried peppers and onions	114	55	216
Rice	176	5	4
Totals for each individual/meal	561	29	434

Fiber per person: (with fish or chicken) about 6½ grams

GAME PLAN

Preheat broiler.

Cook rice.

Prepare onions, garlic and ginger; sauté.

Prepare fish or chicken.

Add peppers to onions.

Cook fish or chicken.

Add soy and vinegar to peppers.

Spread fish or chicken with sauce.

Finish peppers.

Sichuan peanut sauce (F*)   (1 CUP, ENOUGH FOR 14 TO 16 SERVINGS)

Adapted from a recipe used at the Hayes Street Grill in San Francisco.

5 ounces unsweetened chunky peanut butter

2 tablespoons reduced-sodium soy sauce

1½ tablespoons water

2 tablespoons sugar

6 cloves garlic, minced

⅓ bunch fresh coriander (cilantro or Chinese parsley), finely chopped

4 teaspoons hot chili oil

4 to 6 ounces fish fillet, ½ skinned chicken breast or 2 skinned chicken thighs per serving

* The peanut sauce is not actually frozen; it is refrigerated, and keeps for a long time so the main dish is considered one that is done ahead except for the broiling.

Either beat all of the ingredients together in an electric mixer or process all the ingredients but the coriander in a food processor. If using the food processor, just stir in the coriander after it is processed. If it is put all together in the processor, the color will be unappealing.

NOTE TO COOK: This mixture will keep for months in the refrigerator if tightly covered. Use about 1 tablespoon per serving of broiled fish or chicken (4 to 6 ounces of fish fillet; half breast of chicken, skinned; 2 skinned chicken thighs).

Broil fish or chicken and immediately spread with peanut sauce.

Stir-fried peppers and onions   (4 SERVINGS)

2 large onions, thinly sliced
2 large cloves garlic, minced or put through press
2 teaspoons fresh ginger, minced
3 tablespoons corn oil
4 large red and/or green peppers, cut into thin strips

4 teaspoons reduced-sodium soy sauce
4 teaspoons rice vinegar
Freshly ground black pepper to taste

In large skillet sauté onions, garlic and ginger in hot oil for about 2 minutes.

Add pepper strips and continue to cook over medium-high heat for about 5 minutes longer, until peppers begin to soften.

Add soy and vinegar; mix well and cook 1 minute longer. Season with pepper and serve.

Brown rice   (4 SERVINGS)

1 cup brown rice
2 cups water

The night before, or no less than 2 hours before serving, cover the rice with the water and allow to sit in cooking pot.

To serve, bring water and rice to boil, reduce heat and simmer rice in covered pot until tender and water has been absorbed, 17 to 20 minutes.

Chicken breasts with sesame seeds (F)
New potatoes in cumin vinaigrette
Butternut squash with anise
Broiled banana with rum and brown sugar

Add a glass of wine and you increase the calories to 810 and the sodium to 298 milligrams and reduce the fat to 32 percent, or make this a day for a lower-fat breakfast, like a whole-grain cereal and low-fat milk, and a low-fat lunch.

MENU ANALYSIS SUMMARY

	NUTRIENTS PER SERVING		
	CALORIES	% FAT	SODIUM (MG)
Chicken breasts with sesame seeds	276	52	279
New potatoes in cumin vinaigrette	188	43	3
Butternut squash with anise	83	43	4
Broiled banana with rum and brown sugar	150	0	2
Totals for each individual/meal	697	37	288

Fiber per person: about 5½ grams

GAME PLAN

Cook squash.

Cook potatoes.

Dip chicken in sesame seeds.

Prepare salad dressing.

Cook chicken.

Mix dressing.

Drain squash and finish.

Add marinade to chicken.

Cut up potatoes and add to dressing.

After dinner, slice banana in half lengthwise; sprinkle with brown sugar and rum and run under broiler until sugar melts.

Chicken breasts with sesame seeds (F)   (3 SERVINGS)

1½ tablespoons white wine vinegar
1½ tablespoons dry sherry
1 tablespoon reduced-sodium soy sauce
3 large chicken breast halves, skinned and boned

1½ tablespoons sesame seeds
1½ tablespoons corn oil

Combine vinegar, sherry and soy sauce. Place breasts in mixture and freeze.

To serve, defrost. Remove breasts from marinade and dip in sesame seeds. Heat oil in skillet. Brown breasts in hot oil on both sides.

Add marinade; cover and continue cooking until breasts are cooked through, 7 to 10 minutes.

New potatoes in cumin vinaigrette   (3 SERVINGS)

1 pound tiny new potatoes
2 tablespoons olive oil
¼ teaspoon ground cumin

2 tablespoons red wine vinegar
1 clove garlic
Freshly ground black pepper

Scrub potatoes and cook in boiling water until tender, about 20 minutes.

Beat oil with cumin and vinegar in serving bowl. Press garlic clove through press into dressing. Mix with pepper.

When potatoes are ready, drain and cut into halves or quarters directly into serving bowl in which dressing was mixed. Stir with dressing to coat well.

Butternut squash with anise   (3 SERVINGS)

1 pound butternut squash
1 teaspoon anise seed

1 tablespoon unsalted butter

Peel squash; dice or slice and cook in boiling water until soft, about 7 to 10 minutes. Drain.

Place in food processor with anise seed and butter and puree.

Far Eastern chicken
Cumin rice with pignoli
Warm green bean salad

In a way this is a typically American meal. Where else would you find a menu that featured ingredients from the Orient, Italy and France?

MENU ANALYSIS SUMMARY

	NUTRIENTS PER SERVING		
	CALORIES	% FAT	SODIUM (MG)
Far Eastern chicken	283	41	249
Cumin rice with pignoli	387	28	30
Warm green bean salad	76	47	54
Totals for each individual/meal	746	35	333

Fiber per person: almost 6 grams

SHOPPING LIST

Bunch fresh coriander (cilantro or Chinese parsley)

1 small hot green chile (¼ teaspoon)

½ pound skinned, boned chicken breasts

1 ounce pine nuts (2 tablespoons)

Bunch fresh parsley (1½ teaspoons)

½ pound green beans

STAPLES

Onions

Coriander seed

Garlic

Brown sugar

Reduced-sodium soy sauce

Lemon

Oriental sesame paste

Corn oil

Brown rice

Ground cumin

Pepper

Dijon mustard

Dry sherry

White wine vinegar

Hazelnut, walnut or olive oil

GAME PLAN

Soak rice the night before.

Turn on broiler.

Chop onion for rice and sauté in hot oil.

Prepare fresh coriander and chile.

Puree ingredients for chicken.

Add rice to onion with water, cumin and pepper; boil; reduce heat, cover and simmer.

Cut chicken into quarters and place on broiler pan.

Spread with puree.

Put water for green beans on.

Trim green beans.

Broil chicken.

Steam green beans.

Make dressing for beans.

Chop garnish of coriander; chop parsley.

Mix parsley and pignoli with rice.

Mix beans with dressing.

Garnish chicken with coriander.

Far Eastern chicken

(2 SERVINGS)

1 medium onion

1 tablespoon coarsely chopped fresh coriander (cilantro or Chinese parsley)

¼ teaspoon minced fresh hot green chile

½ teaspoon ground coriander seed

1 large clove garlic, halved

¼ teaspoon brown sugar

1½ teaspoons reduced-sodium soy sauce

1½ teaspoons lemon juice

2 teaspoons Oriental sesame paste

½ pound skinned, boned chicken breasts cut into quarters

Additional fresh coriander for garnish

Turn oven or toaster oven to broil.

Chop onion in food processor with steel blade. Chop fresh coriander; mince chile and add with ground coriander, garlic, sugar, soy sauce, lemon juice and sesame paste. Process to puree.

Arrange chicken breasts on broiler pan (if you have a toaster oven that broils, use it) and spread with puree.

Broil 6 inches from heat 12 to 15 minutes.

Chop additional coriander and sprinkle on top of cooked chicken.

Cumin rice with pignoli

¾ cup brown rice
1½ cups water
½ cup chopped onion
1 tablespoon corn oil
1½ teaspoons ground cumin

Freshly ground black pepper to taste
1½ teaspoons finely minced parsley
2 tablespoons pine nuts (pignoli)

Soak rice in water for at least 2 hours, or overnight.
Chop onion.
Heat oil in skillet. Add onion and sauté until it begins to turn golden. Add rice and soaking water along with cumin and pepper. Bring to boil. Reduce heat and cover. Cook rice at simmer about 20 minutes, until rice is tender and water has been absorbed.
Meanwhile, chop parsley.
When rice is cooked, add parsley and pine nuts.

Warm green bean salad

½ pound green beans
1½ teaspoons Dijon mustard
1½ teaspoons dry sherry
1 teaspoon white wine vinegar

1½ teaspoons hazelnut, walnut or olive oil
Freshly ground black pepper to taste

Bring water to boil in steamer.
Trim ends off green beans; wash and steam for about 7 minutes, until tender but still crisp.
In serving bowl beat together mustard, sherry, vinegar and oil. When beans are cooked, stir into dressing. Sprinkle with pepper and serve.

Chicken with coriander
Raisin tabbouleh
Spinach with yogurt and mint

If you want to further reduce the calories in this meal, use chicken breasts instead of chicken thighs. White meat has fewer calories—and less fat—than dark meat.

MENU ANALYSIS SUMMARY

	NUTRIENTS PER SERVING		
	CALORIES	% FAT	SODIUM (MG)
Chicken with coriander	365	47	174
Raisin tabbouleh	474	28	22
Spinach with yogurt and mint	158	34	173
Totals for each individual/meal	997	36	369

Fiber per person: 9 grams

SHOPPING LIST

6 chicken thighs

Bunch fresh coriander (1½ tablespoons)

Bunch scallions (½ cup)

Bunch fresh parsley (6 tablespoons)

¾ pound fresh spinach or ¾ of 10-ounce bag fresh spinach

Few sprigs of fresh mint

STAPLES

Unsalted butter

Onions

No-salt-added tomato puree

Worcestershire sauce

Black pepper

Bulgur

Raisins

Lemon or lime

Corn oil

Sesame oil

Olive oil

Garlic

Plain, low-fat yogurt

Soak bulgur.

Skin chicken and brown in butter.

Slice onions for chicken.

Wash and steam spinach.

Turn chicken and add onions.

Chop onion for spinach and cook in oil.

Chop coriander; mince garlic; chop mint.

Add puree, Worcestershire and

coriander to chicken; season with pepper; cover and cook.

Slice scallions; chop parsley; squeeze lemon juice.

Combine spinach with onion and keep hot.

Drain bulgur and mix with remaining ingredients.

Combine garlic, mint, yogurt and pepper; stir into spinach.

Chicken with coriander

(3 SERVINGS)

6 chicken thighs, skinned

2 tablespoons unsalted butter

2 large onions

1½ tablespoons finely chopped fresh coriander (cilantro or Chinese parsley)

8-ounce can no-salt-added tomato puree

1½ teaspoons Worcestershire sauce

Freshly ground black pepper to taste

Remove skin and exterior fat from chicken thighs. Heat butter in skillet and sauté chicken thighs on one side until golden.

Thinly slice onions, and when chicken is turned to brown on second side, add onions.

Meanwhile, chop coriander and add with puree, Worcestershire and pepper to chicken. Cover, reduce heat and cook until chicken is tender, about 20 minutes.

Raisin tabbouleh

¾ cup bulgur

½ cup sliced scallions

6 tablespoons lightly packed chopped fresh parsley

2 tablespoons freshly squeezed lemon or lime juice

5 tablespoons raisins

1 tablespoon corn oil

1 tablespoon sesame oil

Freshly ground black pepper to taste

Pour boiling water just to cover bulgur in large bowl. Set aside for about 20 minutes, until water is absorbed and bulgur is tender. Drain any excess water and squeeze out remaining water with hands. Slice scallions; chop parsley; squeeze lemon juice. Add to bulger with rest of ingredients and serve.

Spinach with yogurt and mint

¾ pound fresh loose spinach or ¾ of 10-ounce bag fresh spinach

1 medium onion

2 teaspoons olive oil

1 medium clove garlic

1½ teaspoons chopped fresh mint

¾ cup plain, low-fat yogurt

Freshly ground black pepper to taste

Wash spinach; remove tough stems. Drain and steam in the moisture that clings to the leaves.

Chop onion and heat oil. Cook onion in hot oil until translucent. Drain spinach thoroughly, pressing to remove any remaining moisture.

Mince garlic; chop mint and combine with yogurt and pepper to taste. Combine yogurt mixture with onion and spinach. Serve warm, not hot.

Chicken and noodles in sesame-ginger dressing
Tomato wedges

This is a meal for a rich dessert or richer lunch.

MENU ANALYSIS SUMMARY

	NUTRIENTS PER SERVING		
	CALORIES	% FAT	SODIUM (MG)
Chicken and noodles in sesame-ginger dressing	485	20	506
Tomato wedges	45	0	4
Totals for each individual/meal	530	19	510

Fiber per person: 6 grams

SHOPPING LIST

1 large whole chicken breast, skinless and boneless

⅔ pound Kirby or regular cucumbers

Bunch scallions (2)

Bunch fresh coriander leaves (cilantro or Chinese parsley) (2 tablespoons)

8 ounces thin egg noodles

2 medium tomatoes

STAPLES

Oriental sesame paste

Reduced-sodium soy sauce

Sugar

Oriental sesame oil

Hot sesame (chili) oil

Rice vinegar

Fresh ginger

Garlic

White wine or dry vermouth

Boil water for noodles.

Cook chicken.

Cook noodles.

Shred cucumbers.

Drain noodles and run under cold water.

Mince ginger and garlic.

Make sesame paste sauce.

Drain chicken.

Slice scallions.

Mix cucumbers with noodles and scallions.

Shred chicken and mix in with sauce.

Chop coriander and sprinkle over top.

Cut tomatoes.

Chicken and noodles in sesame-ginger dressing   (2 SERVINGS)

1 large whole chicken breast, skinned, boned and halved

Water and white wine or vermouth

8 ounces thin egg noodles

⅔ pound Kirby cucumbers or regular waxed cucumbers

2 cloves garlic

2 scallions

2½ tablespoons Oriental sesame paste

1½ tablespoons reduced-sodium soy sauce

1 teaspoon sugar

1 tablespoon Oriental sesame oil

1 teaspoon hot sesame (chili) oil

1 tablespoon rice vinegar

1 tablespoon white wine or dry vermouth

2 teaspoons minced fresh ginger

2 tablespoons chopped fresh coriander (cilantro or Chinese parsley)

2 medium tomatoes

Cook chicken breasts in a mixture of water and wine or vermouth to cover. Poach until done, about 15 minutes. Cool and drain. Shred.

Cook noodles in 6 quarts boiling water until done, about 2 minutes. Drain and run cold water over noodles. Drain thoroughly.

Coarsely shred cucumbers, peeling if waxed, scrubbing clean and leaving skin on if unwaxed.

Mince ginger and garlic; combine with sesame paste, soy, sugar, sesame oils, rice vinegar, wine; mix thoroughly.

Slice scallions; mix with cucumbers, noodles, and chicken; mix with sauce. Chop coriander; sprinkle on and serve at room temperature. Cut tomatoes into wedges and serve on the side.

65

Grilled "veal" with sauce pizzaiola (F)
Escarole and new potatoes
Orange-onion salad

This menu offers a very large serving of escarole and potatoes.

MENU ANALYSIS SUMMARY

	NUTRIENTS PER SERVING		
	CALORIES	% FAT	SODIUM (MG)
Grilled "veal" with sauce pizzaiola	272	26	661
Escarole and new potatoes	228	28	17
Orange-onion salad	137	33	37
Totals each individual/meal	637	28	715

Fiber per person: a little over 13 grams

GAME PLAN

Cook potatoes.

Preheat broiler.

Prepare onion and garlic for potatoes and sauté.

Prepare escarole.

Prepare spinach for salad.

Grease turkey breasts and broil.

Prepare oranges and onion for salad.

Make salad dressing.

Heat pizzaiola sauce.

Turn breasts.

Add escarole to onions and garlic.

Add potatoes to escarole with chicken broth. Season.

Grilled "veal" with sauce pizzaiola (F) (4 SERVINGS)

The "veal" is in quotation marks because it isn't really veal; it is turkey breasts. Once it's cooked, you cannot tell the difference, and turkey breasts are half the price.

1 tablespoon olive oil
1 medium onion, finely minced
2 large cloves garlic, minced
16-ounce can no-salt-added Italian plum tomatoes, drained and broken up (2 cups)

1 teaspoon dried basil
1 teaspoon dried oregano
4 teaspoons capers, drained

1 pound turkey breasts
Corn oil

Heat oil in large skillet and sauté onion and garlic until onion is wilted. Stir in tomatoes, basil, oregano. Increase heat to medium-high and cook until mixture thickens. Then simmer another 5 minutes. Mix in capers and cook 2 minutes. Mixture should be thick. Freeze in portions suitable for your family's use.

Place turkey breasts on broiler pan lined with foil. Rub oil on breasts. Preheat broiler and broil turkey 3 inches from source of heat, about 4 or 5 minutes on each side, until turkey is cooked through. While turkey is cooking, reheat sauce. Place turkey on serving or individual plates and cover completely with sauce. Serve.

Escarole and new potatoes   (4 LARGE SERVINGS)

1½ pounds small new potatoes
2 tablespoons olive oil
2 medium onions, chopped
2 cloves garlic, minced

1 pound escarole
1 cup chicken broth or stock
Freshly ground black pepper to taste

Cook potatoes in water to cover in covered pot for about 20 minutes, until potatoes are cooked.

Heat oil in large skillet. Sauté onions and garlic in hot oil until onion softens. Meanwhile, wash escarole, drain and break into 2-inch pieces. Add escarole to skillet and stir occasionally until escarole wilts. As potatoes are cooked, add to skillet and cut into quarters (leave skins intact.) Add chicken broth; stir to heat through. Season with pepper and serve.

Orange-onion salad   (4 SERVINGS)

16 fresh spinach leaves
4 navel oranges, peeled and sliced into rounds
3 or 4 very thin slices of red onion, separated into rings

4 teaspoons good-quality red wine vinegar
4 teaspoons good-quality olive oil

Arrange spinach leaves on each of four plates. Arrange orange slices on spinach and slip onion rings between orange slices.

Whisk vinegar and oil together and pour over salads.

SUMMER MENU FOR 4

Meat sauce with pasta or with spaghetti squash (F)
Hot spinach and mushroom salad

With one basic recipe you make two completely different meals. The meat-sauce base is perfect for a picadillo as well, found on page 76.

Spaghetti squash is so named because the flesh acts like strands of spaghetti after it is cooked.

MENU ANALYSIS SUMMARY

	NUTRIENTS PER SERVING		
	CALORIES	% FAT	SODIUM (MG)
Meat sauce with pasta	710	19	94
Meat sauce with spaghetti squash	456	29	95
Hot spinach and mushroom salad	169	43	18
Totals for each individual/meal			
With pasta	879	24	112
With spaghetti squash	625	28	113

Fiber per person: With pasta, 5 grams
With spaghetti squash, 9½ grams

GAME PLAN

Heat water for pasta or prepare spaghetti squash and cook.

Prepare spinach.

Prepare mushrooms and onions and cook in oil.

Cook pasta, if serving.

Heat meat sauce.

Finish salad preparation to point where yogurt is added.

Drain pasta or spaghetti squash.

Add yogurt to spinach salad.

Top spaghetti or squash with meat sauce.

Ground meat base

4 tablespoons corn oil
2 pounds ground turkey
2 large onions, chopped
4 cloves garlic, minced or put through press

6 large ripe tomatoes, coarsely chopped
12-ounce can no-salt-added tomato paste

Heat 2 tablespoons oil in a large frying pan and sauté turkey in it until pink color is gone, stirring to break up pieces. Remove turkey and set to one side. Add remaining oil and sauté onion and garlic in it until onion is limp.

Stir in tomatoes and tomato paste and mix well. Divide mixture in half.

With one half make Meat Sauce; with the other half make Picadillo (page 76).

NOTE TO COOK: Turkey is used instead of ground beef because it has much less fat and fewer calories and once all the other ingredients are mixed in it is difficult to tell whether meat is turkey or beef.

Meat sauce (F)

½ of Ground Meat Base recipe
2 tablespoons chopped fresh oregano or 2 teaspoons dried oregano leaves
1 tablespoon chopped fresh basil or 1 teaspoon dried basil

1 cup dry red wine
Freshly ground black pepper to taste

To the meat base add the remaining ingredients. Simmer 1 hour, until mixture is thick. (If you want a thinner mixture, add 8 ounces of canned tomato puree.)

Freeze in portions suitable for your family's use. To serve, defrost and reheat.

Hot spinach and mushroom salad

1½ pounds loose spinach or 1½ 10-ounce packages cleaned spinach

2 tablespoons corn oil

4 ounces mushrooms, sliced thinly

1 cup diced onions

4 teaspoons freshly squeezed lemon juice

4 teaspoons white vinegar

2 teaspoons sugar

Freshly ground black pepper to taste

2 tablespoons plain, low-fat yogurt

Wash spinach and remove all tough stems. Drain well.

In hot oil sauté mushrooms and onions until onions wilt. Add lemon juice, vinegar, sugar and pepper and mix.

Stir in spinach and cook, only until spinach begins to wilt. Remove from heat; stir in yogurt and serve.

Pasta

3 quarts water

8 ounces thin spaghetti

Bring water to boil in covered pot. Add spaghetti and cook according to package directions, until al dente. Drain and serve with meat sauce.

OR

Spaghetti squash

1 3-pound spaghetti squash

Water

Cut squash in quarters. Remove seeds. Place in pot with enough water to come up just below cut surfaces. Cover and cook over medium-high heat until squash is tender, about 20 minutes. Drain. Serve topped with Meat Sauce.

"Veal" with capers (F)
Braised eggplant
Parslied brown rice

A low-sodium, low-fat meal, good on a day with a higher-fat brunch or a business lunch and a simple breakfast.

MENU ANALYSIS SUMMARY

	NUTRIENTS PER SERVING		
	CALORIES	% FAT	SODIUM (MG)
"Veal" with capers	*652*	*22*	*248*
Braised eggplant	*143*	*63*	*73*
Parslied brown rice	*179*	*5*	*7*
Totals for each individual/meal	*974*	*25*	*328*

Fiber per person: a little over 5 grams

GAME PLAN

Cook rice.

Chop scallions, mince garlic and sauté.

Peel and slice eggplant; add to scallion mixture.

Chop parsley.

Add broth and soy to eggplant; cover and simmer.

Heat "veal."

Stir yogurt into "veal"; season with pepper.

Sprinkle parsley over cooked rice.

"Veal" with capers (F)   (3 SERVINGS)

1 large onion, coarsely chopped

2 tablespoons olive oil

1 teaspoon Hungarian sweet paprika

1 pound boneless turkey breasts, thinly sliced

1 large tomato, cubed

¼ cup dry white wine or vermouth

1½ teaspoons fresh minced rosemary or ½ teaspoon dried rosemary

1 tablespoon capers

2 tablespoons no-salt-added tomato paste

½ cup plain, low-fat yogurt

Freshly ground black pepper to taste

Sauté onion in hot oil with paprika. Add turkey slices and cook quickly until meat loses its color. Add tomato, wine, rosemary and capers. Cook quickly to reduce wine and soften tomato. Stir in tomato paste and heat through. Freeze.

To serve, defrost. Heat slowly; stir in yogurt; season with pepper and heat thoroughly but do not boil or yogurt will separate.

Braised eggplant (3 SERVINGS)

½ cup chopped scallions
2 large cloves garlic, minced
2 tablespoons corn oil
1 pound eggplant, peeled, cut in 3-inch strips, ½ inch wide

½ cup chicken broth
1 to 2 teaspoons reduced-sodium soy sauce

Sauté scallions and garlic in oil for 2 minutes. Add eggplant in single layer in skillet and cook over high heat on both sides until lightly brown. Add broth and soy sauce and cover; simmer 10 to 15 minutes, until eggplant is tender.

Parslied brown rice (3 SERVINGS)

¾ cup brown rice
1½ cups water
Freshly ground black pepper to taste

2 tablespoons chopped fresh parsley

Soak rice in water overnight or for at least two hours in the pot to be used for cooking.

To cook, place pot over high heat and bring to boil. Reduce heat to simmer; cover and cook rice about 20 minutes, until water has evaporated and rice is tender. Season with pepper and sprinkle with parsley.

Ground turkey balls (F)
Zucchini sautéed with fennel
Herbed barley
Fruit Ice

A day to keep the rest of the meals low in calories.

MENU ANALYSIS SUMMARY

	NUTRIENTS PER SERVING		
	CALORIES	% FAT	SODIUM (MG)
Ground turkey balls	325	42	427
Zucchini sautéed with fennel	149	85	2
Herbed barley	304	15	36
¾ cup fruit ice	100	0	0
Totals for each individual/meal	878	34	465

Fiber per person: about 5½ grams

GAME PLAN

Heat oven to 375 degrees.

Chop onion and sauté.

Prepare zucchini.

Add broth, water, barley and thyme to onion; bring to boil.

Sauté zucchini.

Cover barley, reduce heat and simmer.

Bake turkey balls, if frozen.

Chop parsley.

Mince garlic and add to zucchini with other seasonings.

Bake turkey balls, if defrosted.

Sprinkle cooked barley with parsley.

Ground turkey balls (F)   (3 SERVINGS)

2 2½-inch-thick slices dry Italian bread

¾ pound ground raw turkey

¼ pound sweet Italian sausage, casings removed

1 egg and 1 egg white

2¾ tablespoons shredded Gruyère cheese

2 tablespoons minced fresh parsley

Few dashes nutmeg

Freshly ground black pepper to taste

74

Soak bread in water to cover for 5 minutes; squeeze very dry and crumble into bowl with turkey, sausage, eggs, Gruyère, parsley, nutmeg and pepper.

Shape mixture into 10 balls, using about ¼ cup mixture for each ball. Arrange on rack in jelly-roll pan or roasting pan and bake at 350 degrees for 25 minutes or until meat balls are brown and slightly crispy; cool.

Arrange in single layer and freeze in shallow freezer container.

To serve, defrost and bake at 375 degrees for 5 minutes or leave frozen and bake for 15 minutes, or until meat balls are heated through.

Zucchini sautéed with fennel   (3 SERVINGS)

1½ pounds zucchini
3 tablespoons olive oil
1 large clove garlic, minced

¾ teaspoon fennel seeds
1 tablespoon white wine vinegar

Wash zucchini and trim off ends. Cut in half lengthwise and then cut into long strips. Cut each strip into 3 or 4 pieces. Sauté zucchini in hot oil in large skillet until it begins to brown. Add garlic, fennel, vinegar and cook about 5 minutes longer, until zucchini is crisp-tender.

Herbed barley   (3 SERVINGS)

1 medium onion, chopped
1 tablespoon corn oil
10 ounces chicken broth or stock
¾ cup water
1 cup pearl barley

¾ teaspoon dried thyme leaves, crushed
Freshly ground black pepper to taste
1 tablespoon chopped parsley

Sauté onion in hot oil in large saucepan until soft, about 3 minutes. Stir in broth, water, barley and thyme. Bring to boil; reduce heat; cover and simmer for 20 to 25 minutes, or until liquid is absorbed and barley is tender. Season with pepper. Sprinkle with parsley.

Picadillo (F)
Toasted tortillas
Maquechou

This is a higher-calorie meal. For those who keep their total calorie count to 1,500 to 1,800 a day, a salad and/or soup for lunch and a breakfast of a toasted muffin and juice are enough.

MENU ANALYSIS SUMMARY

	NUTRIENTS PER SERVING		
	CALORIES	% FAT	SODIUM (MG)
Picadillo	571	36	509
Toasted tortillas	216	13	66
Maquechou	193	37	18
Totals for each individual/meal	980	31	593

Fiber per person: about 4 grams

GAME PLAN

Heat oven or toaster oven to 500.

Prepare corn and sauté.

Add onion and green pepper.

Heat picadillo.

Season corn.

Heat tortillas.

Beat together yolk and milk.

Grate cheese.

Add milk mixture to corn.

Sprinkle picadillo with cheese.

Picadillo (F)   (4 SERVINGS)

½ of Meat Base recipe (page 70)

2 tablespoons white vinegar

1 teaspoon cinnamon

Scant ⅛ teaspoon ground cloves

1 teaspoon pure chile powder*

½ cup raisins

3-ounce can chopped green chiles, drained

3 tablespoons chopped black olives, packed in brine

⅛ teaspoon ground cumin

Freshly ground black pepper to taste

½ cup coarsely grated sharp cheddar cheese

* Pure chile powder is made from the pepper only. It does not contain other spices and it comes in several strengths from mild to fiery.

To meat base add vinegar, cinnamon, cloves, chile powder, raisins, chiles, olives, cumin and pepper. Heat to boiling; reduce heat and simmer 10 minutes.

Freeze in portions suitable for your family's needs. To serve, defrost, reheat and sprinkle with cheese. Use Toasted Tortillas as wrappers if desired, or just serve tortillas on the side.

Toasted tortillas

(4 SERVINGS)

8 tortillas

Turn oven or toaster oven to 500 degrees. Wrap tortillas in aluminum foil and heat in oven or toaster oven about 10 minutes.

Maquechou

(4 SERVINGS)

This is a Cajun recipe, a version of which I learned from a woman named Enola Prudhomme. Her brother is the renowned Cajun chef Paul Prudhomme.

Kernels from 4 ears of very fresh corn
2 tablespoons unsalted butter
1 large onion, thinly sliced
½ green pepper, finely chopped
Freshly ground black pepper to taste

⅛ teaspoon cayenne pepper
½ egg yolk
6 tablespoons low-fat milk
Sugar (optional)

Scrape kernels from corn. Sauté in hot butter for 2 minutes. Add onion and green pepper and cook over medium-high heat until onion is soft, 5 to 7 minutes. Season with black pepper and cayenne.

Meanwhile, beat yolk half with milk. Add sugar only if corn is not sweet. Stir the milk-yolk mixture into the corn and cook 2 to 3 minutes longer, over medium heat, until mixture thickens slightly.

NOTE TO COOK: If you are using newly picked corn you will need less milk, and if the corn is very sweet you will not need any sugar.

Athenian-style ground meat with tomatoes and scallions (F)

Add a piece of fruit, which adds 100 calories and reduces fat even more.

MENU ANALYSIS SUMMARY

	NUTRIENTS PER SERVING		
	CALORIES	% FAT	SODIUM (MG)
Athenian-style ground meat with tomatoes and scallions	406	44	161
with 1 pita	115	16	148
with 2 pitas	230	16	296
Totals for each individual/meal			
with 1 pita	521	38	309
with 2 pitas	636	34	457

Fiber per person: with 1 pita, about 9 grams; with 2 pitas, about 11 grams

GAME PLAN

Heat sandwich filling.

Prepare cucumbers and mix with yogurt.

Slice tomatoes and scallions.

Heat pitas.

Athenian-style ground meat with tomatoes and scallions with pita (F)   (3 SERVINGS)

1 tablespoon olive oil

1 pound ground raw turkey

1 large onion, chopped

1 large clove garlic, minced

2 large red or green peppers, chopped*

1 teaspoon dried oregano leaves, crushed

1 teaspoon dried thyme leaves, crushed

3 tablespoons good-quality red wine vinegar or red wine

Freshly ground black pepper to taste

1 cup plain, low-fat yogurt

4 small Kirby cucumbers, cubed

3 to 6 large whole-wheat pitas

2 large tomatoes, sliced

6 scallions, thinly sliced

Heat oil in large skillet and sauté turkey in hot oil, breaking up with fork, until meat browns. Add onion, garlic, red peppers, oregano and thyme and cook until onion is soft over medium-low heat. Add vinegar or wine and pepper. Freeze.

To serve, defrost and heat mixture thoroughly. Adjust seasonings. Mix yogurt with cucumbers. Toast pitas and cut in half.

Serve meat topped with cucumbers and yogurt. Serve tomatoes and scallions on the side.

Sandwiches can be made of all the ingredients, using the pita bread. The amount of bread each person desires depends very much on individual capacity.

NOTE TO COOK: This meal is so easy to make, it takes less than thirty minutes and could be a thirty-minute meal, too.

* Red peppers are much sweeter than green peppers and are preferable.

Vegetarian lasagna (F)
Red pepper salad

To increase the calories while reducing the percentage of fat, add some crusty, hearty peasant bread and fruit for dessert.

For a person with a very hearty appetite, a larger portion of lasagna can be served.

MENU ANALYSIS SUMMARY

	NUTRIENTS PER SERVING		
	CALORIES	% FAT	SODIUM (MG)
Vegetarian lasagna	485	22	454
Red pepper salad	92	61	13
Totals for each individual/meal	577	30	467

Fiber per person: about 6½ grams

GAME PLAN

Heat oven to 375 degrees.

Prepare peppers, mushrooms and scallions for salad.

Bake lasagna.

Make salad dressing and toss with vegetables.

Vegetarian lasagna (F)   (4 SERVINGS)

16 ounces no-salt-added canned tomatoes

12 ounces no-salt-added tomato sauce

½ teaspoon dried oregano

½ teaspoon dried basil

Freshly ground black pepper to taste

1 tablespoon olive oil

2 large onions, chopped

1 large clove garlic, minced

6 ounces mushrooms, chopped

1 large carrot, scraped and chopped

½ green pepper, chopped

8 ounces lasagna noodles

3 ounces Parmesan or other sharp Italian cheese, grated

5 ounces skim milk mozzarella, sliced

6 ounces low-fat (1% fat) cottage cheese

Simmer tomatoes, tomato sauce, oregano, basil and pepper while you prepare other ingredients.

Heat oil in skillet and sauté onions and garlic until onion is limp. Add mushrooms, carrot and green pepper and sauté over high heat to evaporate liquid quickly.

Cook lasagna noodles according to package directions.

When vegetables are softened, combine with tomato mixture and simmer another 15 minutes, longer if you are still preparing the other ingredients.

To assemble: Cover the bottom of a 12 × 8 × 2 freezer-to-oven-to-table casserole with several spoonfuls of sauce. Crisscross layers of noodles, spread with half of cheeses, then with noodles. Spread with remaining cottage cheese, Parmesan and all of sauce. Top with remaining mozzarella. Or divide ingredients in half and assemble in two smaller casseroles.

Wrap and freeze. To serve, defrost and bake at 375 degrees for 30 minutes for large one, 20 to 25 minutes for small.

NOTE: The sauce is good with plain pasta.

Red pepper salad
(4 SERVINGS)

2 tablespoons olive oil
2 tablespoons red or white wine vinegar
½ teaspoon dried basil
¼ teaspoon dried oregano
Freshly ground black pepper to taste

2 large red peppers, cut into julienne strips
8 medium mushrooms, sliced
4 large scallions, thinly sliced

Beat oil and vinegar with wire whisk or fork. Beat in basil, oregano and pepper.

Add vegetables to dressing. Stir well.

NOTE TO COOK: If red peppers are unavailable, green may be used, but the salad will not be as sweet.

Fragrant brown rice (F)
Radish and cheese salad
Spiced zucchini

Before you turn up your nose at the radishes, try this salad. I am not a radish fancier, but this is just delicious because of the combination with the cheese.

MENU ANALYSIS SUMMARY

	NUTRIENTS PER SERVING		
	CALORIES	% FAT	SODIUM (MG)
Fragrant brown rice	497	18	41
Radish and cheese salad	96	65	71
Spiced zucchini	112	64	5
Totals for each individual/meal	705	29	117

Fiber per person: about 6½ grams

GAME PLAN

Prepare zucchini and sauté.

Prepare radishes and scallions.

Make salad dressing.

Add tomato and seasonings to zucchini.

Heat brown rice.

Grate cheese and add to dressing with radishes and scallions.

Add cashews to rice and heat through.

Fragrant brown rice (F)

(3 SERVINGS)

1 cup brown rice

2 cups water

2 large onions, sliced

1 clove garlic, minced or put through press

2 tablespoons corn oil

12 medium mushrooms, sliced (¼ pound)

2 teaspoons minced fresh ginger

½ cup raisins

½ teaspoon ground cardamom

¼ teaspoon ground cloves

½ teaspoon ground cinnamon

⅛ to ¼ teaspoon cayenne

Freshly ground black pepper to taste

1 cup vegetable broth

2 ounces unsalted roasted cashews

Cover rice with water and bring to boil; reduce heat to simmer; cover and cook rice about 45 minutes, or until tender and water has evaporated.

Sauté onions and garlic in hot oil until onions are soft, about 5 minutes. Add mushrooms, ginger, raisins and spices to onions. Continue sautéing until mushrooms are soft.

Stir vegetables into cooked rice with broth. Freeze.

To serve, defrost and cook over moderate heat, until mixture is hot throughout. Add cashews and cook another minute.

Radish and cheese salad (3 SERVINGS)

6 ounces radishes without their tops (8 ounces with tops)

2 large scallions

1 teaspoon Dijon mustard or, if desired, mustard flavored with basil or tarragon

1 tablespoon olive oil

1 tablespoon plus 2 teaspoons red wine vinegar (preferably balsamic)

3 tablespoons coarsely grated sharp cheese, well packed

Freshly ground black pepper to taste

Trim, wash and thinly slice radishes. Slice scallions thinly.

Combine mustard with oil and vinegar and mix well. Stir in radish slices, onions and cheese and mix well. Season with pepper.

Spiced zucchini (3 SERVINGS)

1¼ pounds zucchini, sliced ¼ inch thick

1½ tablespoons corn oil

1 large tomato, diced, or 6 ounces no-salt-added tomato puree

¾ teaspoon ground cumin

¾ teaspoon ground coriander

Freshly ground black pepper to taste

In large skillet sauté zucchini in oil 5 to 7 minutes, until golden on both sides.

Add tomato and seasonings; bring to boil and reduce heat. Cover and simmer until zucchini is tender, about 5 minutes.

Broiled eggplant, cheese and tomato sauce (F)
Green noodles
Greens with buttermilk dressing

A very low-calorie meal that can be increased with the addition of some whole-grain Italian bread, which will also sop up some of the sauce with the eggplant.

MENU ANALYSIS SUMMARY

	NUTRIENTS PER SERVING		
	CALORIES	% FAT	SODIUM (MG)
Broiled eggplant, cheese and tomato sauce	325	36	378
Green noodles	210	0	2
Greens with buttermilk dressing	68	13	87
Totals for each individual/meal	603	22	467

Fiber per person: a little over 6 grams

GAME PLAN

Heat oven.

Boil water for noodles in covered pot.

Bake eggplant.

Prepare salad.

Cook noodles.

Broiled eggplant, cheese and tomato sauce (F)   (3 SERVINGS)

One of those miraculous recipes in which the eggplant is broiled, not sautéed. This browns it, partially cooks it and keeps it completely free of oil, which sautéed eggplant just loves to soak up.

1 large eggplant, about 1¼ pounds

SAUCE:

1 tablespoon olive oil

1 clove garlic, minced

1 large onion, chopped

4 ounces mushrooms, thinly sliced

4 ounces sharp cheese, such as cheddar or provolone, very thinly sliced

2 tablespoons parsley, chopped

½ teaspoon oregano

1 teaspoon basil

28-ounce can no-salt-added tomato puree

Freshly ground black pepper

Wash eggplant and slice off both ends. Slice remaining eggplant into ½-inch-thick round slices and place on broiler pan under broil. Broil on each side until eggplant slices are browned. Watch carefully. Total broiling time is about 10 minutes.

Meanwhile heat oil in large skillet and sauté onion and garlic in hot oil until onion softens. Add mushrooms and sauté 1 or 2 minutes longer. Add parsley, oregano, basil and puree. Cook over low heat 5 minutes or longer, until eggplant is ready. Season with pepper.

Arrange eggplant slices in a single layer in shallow ovenproof baking dish. Top with cheese slices and cover with tomato sauce. Wrap for freezer. Freeze.

To serve, defrost. Bake, uncovered, at 450 degrees for 15 to 20 minutes, until sauce is bubbling.

Serve over green noodles.

NOTE TO COOK: If eggplant is not at room temperature, it will take longer to heat through. Reduce heat to 400 and bake longer, 25 to 30 minutes.

Green noodles (3 SERVINGS)

6 ounces green noodles

Bring 3 quarts water to boil in covered pot. Add noodles and cook, uncovered, until noodles are tender, according to package directions. Drain and serve with sauce from eggplant.

Greens with buttermilk dressing (3 SERVINGS)

6 ounces mixed greens such as Boston and red lettuce, mache or arugula
⅓ cup low-fat buttermilk
1 teaspoon Dijon mustard
1½ tablespoons grated cucumber

⅓ of 1 scallion, thinly sliced
1½ teaspoons chopped fresh parsley
Freshly ground black pepper to taste

Mix or shake dressing ingredients well to blend. Serve over greens.

Kasha, corn and cheese casserole (F)
Apple-walnut salad with chutney-yogurt dressing

Kasha, also known as buckwheat groats, is a familiar product to Jews and Russians. It has a distinctive nutty taste and is a delightful alternative to rice.

MENU ANALYSIS SUMMARY

	NUTRIENTS PER SERVING		
	CALORIES	% FAT	SODIUM (MG)
Kasha, corn and cheese casserole	275	33	329
Apple-walnut salad with chutney-yogurt dressing	215	29	60
Totals for each individual/meal	490	31	389

Fiber per person: a little over 11 grams

GAME PLAN

Mix salad dressing.

Heat kasha casserole.

Prepare lettuce, apples and walnuts.

Top casserole with cheese; melt cheese.

Mix salad ingredients with dressing.

Kasha, corn and cheese casserole (F)   (4 SERVINGS)

1 large onion, chopped

1 tablespoon corn oil

1 egg white

1 cup whole-grain buckwheat groats (kasha)

2 cups water

2 teaspoons dried oregano

¾ teaspoon ground cumin

1¼ teaspoons pure chile powder*

½ cup low-fat, no-salt-added cottage cheese

12-ounce can whole-kernel corn

Freshly ground black pepper to taste

4 tablespoons tightly packed, coarsely grated sharp cheddar cheese

* See footnote on page 76.

Sauté onion in hot oil until tender. Mix egg white with groats thoroughly and add to onion, stirring to separate each grain. Add water, oregano, cumin and chile powder. Bring to boil. Lower heat, cover and cook about 10 minutes, until liquid is almost completely absorbed and groats are almost tender.

Mix in corn and cottage cheese. Season with pepper.

Freeze, if desired, in portions suitable for your family's use. To serve, defrost; heat over low heat. Top with cheese, cover and cook for 2 minutes more to melt cheese, or run under broiler to melt cheese and brown.

Apple-walnut salad with chutney-yogurt dressing

(4 SERVINGS)

⅔ cup plain, low-fat yogurt

8 teaspoons (2 tablespoons plus 2 teaspoons) mango chutney

1 teaspoon Dijon mustard

4 heads Bibb lettuce or equivalent amount Boston lettuce

3 large apples

4 tablespoons chopped walnuts
 Freshly ground black pepper to taste

Mix yogurt with chutney and mustard.

Wash, drain and dry lettuce. Wash apples, dry and core. Cut into small cubes.

Mix lettuce, apples and walnuts with dressing and season with black pepper.

Tomato sauce Provençal (F)
Pasta
Spinach-almond salad

This meal is so low in fat, it's perfect for the day you have a high-fat lunch or following one of those elaborate Sunday brunches.

You could also sprinkle 2 tablespoons of freshly grated Parmesan cheese on the pasta and still have a low-fat meal.

MENU ANALYSIS SUMMARY

	NUTRIENTS PER SERVING		
	CALORIES	% FAT	SODIUM (MG)
Tomato sauce Provençal	201	4	49
Pasta	210–319	0	2–3
Spinach-almond salad	105	26	86
Totals for each individual/meal	516–625	12–10	137–138

Fiber per person: a little over 6½ grams

GAME PLAN

Boil water in covered pot for spaghetti.

Prepare spinach, mushrooms and almonds for salad.

Combine dressing ingredients.

Cook spaghetti.

Heat sauce Provençal.

Cook salad dressing.

Drain spaghetti.

Toss dressing with salad.

Water

Tomato sauce Provençal (F) (ABOUT 8 CUPS, 4 SERVINGS WITH PASTA)

6 pounds fresh tomatoes or 3 28-ounce cans no-salt-added tomatoes

2 tablespoons olive oil

1 large onion, finely diced

5 medium cloves garlic, mashed

3 1-inch-long pieces orange peel without the white

2 sprigs fresh parsley

1 bay leaf

2 sprigs fresh thyme or ¼ teaspoon dried thyme

½ teaspoon fennel seeds

1½ teaspoons chopped fresh basil leaf (about 3 large leaves) or ½ teaspoon dried basil

¼ teaspoon ground coriander seed

Freshly ground pepper to taste

¼ teaspoon celery seed

6-ounce can no-salt-added tomato paste

2 or 3 ounces spaghetti per serving

Plunge fresh tomatoes into boiling water for a few seconds and remove skins. Chop pulp coarsely, if using fresh tomatoes.

Heat oil in heavy pot; add onion and cook slowly about 15 minutes, until onion is transparent. Add remaining ingredients and simmer for 1½ to 2 hours, stirring occasionally. Break up tomatoes as they cook.

Remove parsley, bay leaf and orange peel. Freeze in portions suitable for your family's use.

To serve, defrost, reheat, adjust seasonings.

Cook spaghetti, allowing 2 or 3 ounces dried pasta per serving. Serve sauce over drained spaghetti.

NOTE: To make meat sauce from this recipe, combine 4 cups of sauce with ½ pound ground beef that has been cooked in its own fat until the pink color has turned brown. Pour off excess fat; add beef to cooked onions with the other ingredients.

If you want to further reduce the calories for a dieter, serve half of a small cooked spaghetti squash instead of the pasta with the sauce.

Spinach-almond salad

(4 SERVINGS)

4 cups spinach leaves

¼ pound mushrooms, sliced

2 tablespoons toasted sliced almonds

2 tablespoons olive oil

2 tablespoons tarragon vinegar

½ teaspoon crushed tarragon

⅛ teaspoon nutmeg

Freshly ground black pepper to taste

Remove tough stems from spinach; wash and dry and tear into bite-size pieces. Place in serving bowl with mushrooms and almonds.

Combine remaining ingredients in saucepan and heat to boiling. Pour hot dressing over salad and toss. Serve.

Vegetable curry with tofu (F)
Brown rice
Spinach salad with soy dressing

NOTE: To increase calories, add fruit for dessert, whole-grain bread with the salad.

MENU ANALYSIS SUMMARY

	NUTRIENTS PER SERVING		
	CALORIES	% FAT	SODIUM (MG)
Vegetable curry with tofu	388	41	98
Brown rice	234	4	6
Spinach salad with soy dressing	59	15	244
Total for each individual/meal	681	26	348

Fiber per person: 9½ grams

GAME PLAN

Cook brown rice.

Prepare spinach.

Heat curry.

Make salad dressing and toss with spinach.

Chop coriander.

Add yogurt to curry; heat.

Sprinkle curry with coriander.

Vegetable curry with tofu (F)   (3 SERVINGS)

1 pound butternut squash
1 pound zucchini
1 large clove garlic
   1-inch piece fresh ginger
1 large onion
2 tablespoons corn oil
½ pound tofu, diced
2 teaspoons curry powder

¼ cup sunflower seeds (unsalted)
¼ cup raisins
   Freshly ground black pepper

1½ cups plain, low-fat yogurt
2 tablespoons chopped fresh
   coriander (cilantro or Chinese
   parsley)

Peel butternut squash and slice with thin slicer blade in processor. Steam for 5 minutes, or until crisp-tender.

Wash the zucchini and slice with thin slicer blade of food processor.

Mince garlic and ginger in food processor with steel blade. Then chop onion coarsely.

Heat oil in large skillet and sauté onion-garlic-ginger mixture over medium heat for 3 or 4 minutes, until onion is softened. Add zucchini and sauté 3 to 5 minutes more. Then add tofu and curry, squash, sunflower seeds and raisins and cook over low heat for 5 minutes. Season with pepper.

Freeze before adding yogurt and coriander.

To serve, defrost and heat through; stir in yogurt; heat through and sprinkle on coriander. Do not boil or yogurt will separate.

Brown rice   (3 SERVINGS)

1 cup brown rice   2 cups water

The night before or no less than 2 hours before serving, cover the rice with the water and allow to sit in cooking pot.

To serve, bring water and rice to boil; reduce heat and simmer rice in covered pot until tender and water is absorbed, 17 to 20 minutes.

Spinach salad with soy dressing   (3 SERVINGS)

4 cups fresh loose spinach   2 teaspoons red wine vinegar
2 teaspoons reduced-sodium soy   4 teaspoons dry sherry
  sauce
2 tablespoons corn oil

Wash spinach; remove tough stems; drain and dry. With wire whisk, beat soy sauce with oil, vinegar and sherry.

Place spinach in large bowl and toss with dressing, mixing well to coat leaves.

Chili (F)
Red pepper and cucumber salad
Corn tortillas

This is chili without the carne. If you want the meat, you have it on the side.

MENU ANALYSIS SUMMARY

	NUTRIENTS PER SERVING		
	CALORIES	% FAT	SODIUM (MG)
Chili	275	26	176
Red pepper and cucumber salad	96	65	12
Corn tortillas	216	4	16
Totals for each individual/meal	587	25	204

Fiber per person: 12 grams

GAME PLAN

Set oven or toaster oven at 500 degrees.

Whisk dressing.

Wrap tortillas in foil and place in oven.

Heat chili.

Prepare peppers and cucumbers.

Finish salad.

Chili (F) (4 TO 5 SERVINGS)

1 pound plum tomatoes
2 tablespoons corn oil
2 large onions, chopped
3 large cloves garlic, minced
1 green pepper, chopped
1 jalapeño pepper, minced
2 cups canned no-salt-added tomato puree
¼ teaspoon ground coriander seed
⅛ teaspoon allspice

1½ teaspoons dried oregano
1 tablespoon mild pure chile powder
1½ teaspoons ground cumin
2 tablespoons fresh coriander (cilantro or Chinese parsley) (optional)
2 16-ounce cans pinto or kidney beans or ½ to ⅔ cups dried beans, cooked

8 to 10 corn tortillas

Chop half the tomatoes; puree the rest. (Use food processor if you have one.)

Heat oil; sauté onion, garlic, green pepper and jalapeño until onion is soft; add tomatoes, tomato puree, spices and beans. Cover and simmer about 30 minutes; adjust seasonings.

Freeze in portions suitable for your family's use. To serve, defrost and reheat. Serve with corn tortillas, wrapped in foil and warmed in toaster oven at 500 degrees for 10 minutes.

Red pepper and cucumber salad (4 SERVINGS)

2 tablespoons red wine vinegar
2 tablespoons olive oil
2 scallions, thinly sliced
2 large red bell peppers, cut in julienne strips
4 Kirby cucumbers, scrubbed, or

2 regular peeled cucumbers, cut into batons
Freshly ground black pepper to taste
2 tablespoons chopped fresh chives

Whisk vinegar with oil in salad bowl and stir in scallions. Add red peppers and cucumbers; toss with pepper. Sprinkle with chives and serve.

Creamy basil sauce
Linguine
Tomato and red onion relish

You can afford a rich dessert.

MENU ANALYSIS SUMMARY

	NUTRIENTS PER SERVING		
	CALORIES	% FAT	SODIUM (MG)
Creamy basil sauce			
with pine nuts	258	28	245
without pine nuts	216	12	215
Linguine	319	0	3
Tomato and red onion relish	144	44	10
Totals for each individual/meal			
with pine nuts	721	19	258
without pine nuts	679	15	228

Fiber per person: about 4½ grams

SHOPPING LIST

6 ounces linguine

¾ cup low-fat, no-salt-added cottage cheese

1 ounce sweet Gorgonzola

1 bunch fresh basil (1¼ cups)

5-ounce tomato plus 1 pound tomatoes

1 medium red onion (1 cup)

1 ounce pine nuts (2 tablespoons) (optional)

STAPLES

Garlic

Black pepper

Olive oil

Red wine vinegar

Boil water.

Process garlic; add cheeses and basil.

Add tomato.

Cook pasta.

Prepare salad.

Season pasta sauce; add optional pine nuts.

Drain pasta and mix with sauce.

Creamy basil sauce for linguine

(2 SERVINGS)

6 ounces linguine

1 large clove garlic

¾ cup low-fat, no-salt-added cottage cheese

1 ounce sweet Gorgonzola

1¼ cups lightly packed fresh basil leaves

5-ounce ripe tomato

Freshly ground black pepper to taste

2 tablespoons pine nuts (optional)

Bring 3 quarts water to boil in covered pot. Add linguine and cook until al dente.

Chop garlic in food processor. Add the cottage cheese, Gorgonzola and basil and process until smooth. Add tomato, cut in chunks, and process only until tomatoes are tiny chunks. Stir in pepper and pine nuts, if used.

When pasta is cooked, drain well and stir into sauce. Serve immediately.

NOTE TO COOK: This is a remarkable sauce because it tastes so creamy and yet is made with a low-fat cottage cheese.

Pine nuts are optional. They add a nice crunch, but they also add 42 calories and 5 percent fat.

Tomato and red onion relish

(2 SERVINGS)

2 ripe tomatoes, approximately 1 pound

1 cup chopped red onion

1 tablespoon olive oil

1 tablespoon red wine vinegar

Freshly ground black pepper to taste

Cut tomatoes into small dice; chop red onion and mix. Stir in oil and vinegar and mix gently but thoroughly. Sprinkle with pepper and serve.

Hot potato and broccoli vinaigrette
Carrots with orange and cardamom
Sourdough rolls with blue cheese
Fruit

Low calories but moderate amounts of fat. In order to increase calories without adding fat, add more fruit, more rolls.

MENU ANALYSIS SUMMARY

	NUTRIENTS PER SERVING		
	CALORIES	% FAT	SODIUM (MG)
Hot potato and broccoli vinaigrette	277	59	21
Carrots with orange and cardamom	101	44	43
Sourdough rolls with blue cheese	199	32	410
Fruit	50	0	0
Totals for each individual/meal	627	36	474

Fiber per person: a little over 11 grams

SHOPPING LIST

1 pound tiny new potatoes
1 pound broccoli
Bunch scallions (2)
1 pound carrots
1 medium eating orange

2 ounces soft young blue cheese (Saga, Italian sweet Gorgonzola, 3 tablespoons)
4 heat-and-serve sourdough rolls (6 ounces)

STAPLES

Olive oil
Cider vinegar
Garlic
Dry mustard

Paprika
Black pepper
Unsalted butter
Cardamom

GAME PLAN

Cook potatoes.

Heat water for broccoli.

Prepare and cook broccoli.

Peel and slice carrots; sauté with cardamom.

Squeeze orange juice.

Make salad dressing.

Prepare rolls and cheese mixture.

Heat toaster oven or oven broiler.

Broil bread.

Add orange to carrots.

Drain potatoes; cut in quarters and add to dressing in bowl.

Hot potato and broccoli vinaigrette (4 SERVINGS)

1 pound tiny new potatoes

1 pound broccoli, trimmed of tough stems, heads cut into florets

1 clove garlic

2 scallions

4 tablespoons olive oil

4 tablespoons cider vinegar

½ teaspoon dry mustard

¼ teaspoon paprika

Freshly ground black pepper to taste

Scrub potatoes and cook whole in their jackets in covered pot in water to cover until tender, about 20 minutes. Cut in quarters.

Steam broccoli over hot water until just tender, about 7 minutes.

While potatoes and broccoli cook, press garlic, slice scallions finely; combine with remaining ingredients and whisk.

Place quartered potatoes (do not peel them) and broccoli in serving dish and pour over dressing. Stir gently and serve warm.

Carrots with orange and cardamom

1 pound carrots
1 medium eating orange
¼ to ½ teaspoon ground
   cardamom

1½ tablespoons unsalted butter
   Freshly ground black pepper
   to taste

Peel carrots.

Using the thinnest slicer of a food processor, slice peeled carrots. Sauté carrots with cardamom in hot butter for about 15 minutes. Squeeze orange on orange juice squeezer, reserving both juice and pulp. Add to carrots. Season with pepper and cook until tender.

Sourdough rolls with blue cheese

4 heat-and-serve sourdough
   rolls, about 1½ ounces each
3 tablespoons soft blue cheese,

   such as Saga or Italian sweet
   Gorgonzola

Split rolls and spread each cut side with 1½ teaspoons blue cheese.

Broil in toaster oven or under broiler for about 7 minutes, until cheese is melted and bread is turning golden brown. Serve warm, not hot.

Fresh tomato sauce with rotini
Corn and green pepper salad
Green onion and cheese bread

This is a day to eat a low-fat breakfast and lunch: cereal with skim milk, juice, toast and jelly but no butter. For lunch, soup, chicken without skin, poached fish, tuna with yogurt dressing (no oils, butter, mayonnaise, etc.).

MENU ANALYSIS SUMMARY

	NUTRIENTS PER SERVING		
	CALORIES	% FAT	SODIUM (MG)
Fresh tomato sauce with rotini	467	48	205
Corn and green pepper salad	154	0	15
Green onion and cheese bread	208	43	225
Totals for each individual/meal	829	38	445

Fiber per person: about 9 grams

SHOPPING LIST

2 pounds ripe tomatoes
1 bunch fresh basil (⅔ cup)
Bunch fresh parsley (¼ cup)
Few sprigs fresh oregano leaves (2 tablespoons) (optional)
1½ pounds rotini
4 ounces Parmesan
4 or 5 large ears corn

1 large green pepper
Small red onion (6 tablespoons)
Green chile (1 fresh or from can) (1 tablespoon)
½ pound sourdough, French or Italian bread
Bunch scallions (2)

STAPLES

Garlic
Olive oil
Black pepper
Dried oregano

White vinegar (or malt)
Sugar
Ground cumin
Unsalted butter

Take butter out of refrigerator.

Put on water for corn.

Put on water for pasta.

Shuck corn.

Make tomato sauce.

Cook corn.

Turn on broiler.

Drain corn and cool.

Scrape kernels off ears.

Cut up green pepper, onion and chile.

Cook pasta.

Grate cheese for tomato sauce and for bread.

Cut up scallions and mix with cheese and butter; spread on bread; broil.

Mix corn with remaining salad ingredients.

Drain pasta; mix with tomato sauce; sprinkle with cheese.

Fresh tomato sauce with rotini

(ENOUGH FOR 1½ POUNDS PASTA, 4 SERVINGS)

2 pounds red ripe tomatoes

2 tablespoons coarsely chopped fresh oregano leaves or 2 teaspoons dried leaves

¼ cup coarsely chopped fresh parsley

4 cloves garlic

⅔ cup fresh basil leaves, tightly packed

⅓ cup good-quality olive oil

Freshly ground black pepper to taste

1½ pounds rotini

1 cup finely grated fresh Parmesan cheese

Bring 6 quarts water to a boil in covered pot for pasta.

Cut up tomatoes into large chunks. Squeeze out seeds. Chop oregano and parsley. Add half of all the ingredients but the rotini and cheese to food processor or blender and blend until smooth. Set aside. Add remaining half of ingredients (except rotini and cheese) and blend until smooth. Combine processed ingredients.

Sauce can be served immediately or can ripen in the refrigerator for several hours or overnight.

To serve, cook rotini (spiral macaroni of any kind is recommended because it holds the sauce well). Grate Parmesan. Drain rotini and serve while piping hot, with cold sauce. Sprinkle with Parmesan.

Corn and green pepper salad

3 cups fresh corn kernels (about 4 or 5 large ears)

1 cup finely chopped green pepper

6 tablespoons minced red onion

1 tablespoon chopped green chile from a can with liquid or fresh chile, chopped (optional)

4 tablespoons malt or white vinegar

2 teaspoons sugar

1 teaspoon ground cumin

Freshly ground black pepper to taste

Boil water. Shuck corn and cook in boiling water for 1 minute. Cool corn by running under cold water.

Scrape kernels off ears.

Cut green pepper, mince red onion and chop chile.

Mix corn kernels with green pepper, onion, vinegar, sugar, cumin, black pepper and optional chile.

Scallion and cheese bread

8 ounces sourdough, French or Italian bread

2 scallions

3 tablespoons unsalted butter

2 tablespoons freshly grated Parmesan cheese

Turn on toaster oven or oven to broil.

Cut loaf of bread in half, lengthwise.

Cut scallions into thin rings.

Grate cheese.

Combine scallions, cheese, butter and spread on bread.

Toast in toaster oven or under broiler until cheese and butter have melted and bread is beginning to brown.

Fish under a bed of ratatouille (F)
Boiled new potatoes

Treat yourself to a rich dessert. Have a brownie or two chocolate chip cookies. One of only two frozen-fish dishes in the book.

MENU ANALYSIS SUMMARY

	NUTRIENTS PER SERVING		
	CALORIES	% FAT	SODIUM (MG)
Fish under a bed of ratatouille	438	4	302
Boiled new potatoes	126	almost 0	5
Totals for each individual/meal	564	3	307

Fiber per person: about 7 grams

GAME PLAN

Cook potatoes.

Turn on oven.

Bake fish.

Chop fresh coriander.

Drain cooked potatoes.

Sprinkle cooked fish with coriander.

Fish under a bed of ratatouille (F)   (2 SERVINGS)

2 teaspoons lime juice

1 pound red snapper or other fish fillets or steaks

5 or 6 cups ratatouille base (page 47)

1 tablespoon mild chile powder*

⅛ teaspoon cinnamon

3 tablespoons dry sherry

Freshly ground black pepper to taste

Fresh coriander (cilantro or Chinese parsley) or parsley for garnish

* Chile powder is the pure pepper, no other spices added. It comes in several strengths from mild to hot.

Squeeze lime juice over fish.

Combine ratatouille base with chile, cinnamon, sherry and black pepper.

Place fish in shallow baking dish in single layer. Top with ratatouille, making sure fish is covered. Freeze.

To serve, defrost and cover. Bake at 400 degrees for 10 to 15 minutes, depending on thickness of fish.

Sprinkle with chopped fresh coriander if available, or parsley.

Boiled new potatoes   (2 SERVINGS)

10 ounces tiny new potatoes   Water

Scrub potatoes, but do not peel. Place in pot with water to cover. Bring to boil, covered, and boil 15 to 20 minutes, depending on size of potatoes, until tender. Drain and serve with fish.

Shrimp sesame (F)
Angel hair pasta
Orange and red pepper salad

There are almost no fish dishes that I think freeze well. The fish usually becomes tough and/or watery. But the coating of the shrimp with the sauce appears to prevent either of those problems and so offers one of the few really good frozen-fish dishes in the book.

MENU ANALYSIS SUMMARY

	NUTRIENTS PER SERVING		
	CALORIES	% FAT	SODIUM (MG)
Shrimp sesame	311	41	628
Angel hair pasta	210	0	2
Orange and red pepper salad	147	43	40
Totals for each individual/meal	668	28	670

Fiber per person: a little over 6 grams

GAME PLAN

Boil water for pasta.

Prepare oranges and peppers for salad.

Cook pasta.

Prepare salad dressing and mix with oranges and peppers.

Heat shrimp mixture.

Shrimp sesame with angel hair pasta (F) (4 SERVINGS)

2 pounds shrimp in the shell
2 tablespoons sesame oil
2 large cloves garlic, minced
4 large stalks celery, finely cut
½ pound lean ground pork
½ cup thinly sliced scallions
1½ cups beef stock

3 tablespoons reduced-sodium soy sauce
6 tablespoons dry sherry
2 teaspoons minced fresh ginger
1½ teaspoons hot sesame oil

½ pound angel hair pasta

Peel shrimp and cut in half. Heat sesame oil; cook garlic and celery until soft. Add pork and scallions and cook until pork is brown.

Add shrimp, stock, soy sauce, sherry, ginger and hot sesame oil and stir. Freeze in portions suitable for your family's use.

To serve, defrost.

Cook pasta according to package directions.

Cook shrimp mixture quickly, just until shrimp is pink. Do not overcook.

Mix shrimp sauce with cooked noodles and serve.

NOTE TO COOK: A very thin pasta is essential so that it will absorb the sauce ingredients.

Orange and red pepper salad (4 SERVINGS)

2 tablespoons good-quality olive oil
2 tablespoons red wine vinegar (preferably balsamic)
2 teaspoons Dijon mustard

4 eating oranges, peeled, sections cut in half or quarters
2 large red peppers, cut in julienne strips

Whisk oil with vinegar and mustard. Stir in oranges and pepper and serve.

Steamed sole with dill
Braised potatoes
Curried tomatoes and onion
Fruit ice

To compensate for the high percentage of fat in the tomato dish, bread (without butter) and fruit ice (made without milk products) have been added to the meal, substantially reducing fat.

MENU ANALYSIS SUMMARY

	NUTRIENTS PER SERVING		
	CALORIES	% FAT	SODIUM (MG)
Steamed sole with dill	173	21	112
Braised potatoes	124	43	119
Curried tomatoes and onion	82	87	13
2 slices French bread	110	0	110
¾ cup fruit ice	100	0	0
Totals for each individual/meal	589	28	354

Fiber per person: almost 5 grams

SHOPPING LIST

½ pound sole or flounder fillet
Bunch fresh dill (1 tablespoon)
1 pound tomatoes
1 pound potatoes
Tamari (1 teaspoon)

French bread (4 slices)
Fruit ice
1 ounce Parmesan cheese (2 tablespoons)

STAPLES

Olive oil
Black pepper
Dry sherry
Lemon
Corn oil

Onion
Garlic
Curry powder
Chicken stock
Fresh ginger

Preheat oven, cover pan with foil and arrange fish.

Peel potatoes, cube and cook in hot oil.

Chop onions and garlic and sauté.

Chop tomatoes and mince ginger.

Make sauce for fish and spread over fish; cover with foil.

Add chicken stock to potatoes and cook.

Add tomatoes and remaining ingredients to onions.

Grate cheese.

Steam fish.

Sprinkle cheese over potatoes.

Steamed sole with dill
(2 SERVINGS)

1 teaspoon olive oil
½ pound sole or flounder fillets
　Freshly ground pepper to taste
1 tablespoon chopped fresh dill

1½ teaspoons dry sherry
1 tablespoon lemon juice
1 teaspoon tamari

Preheat oven or toaster oven to 400 degrees. Coat a foil-covered pan with oil and place fillets in single layer on foil. Season with pepper.

Chop dill; combine with sherry, lemon juice and tamari and sprinkle over fillets. Cover pan with foil and bake 5 minutes.

Braised potatoes
(2 SERVINGS)

2 large potatoes, about 1 pound
1 tablespoon olive oil
½ cup hot chicken stock

　Freshly ground black pepper to taste
2 tablespoons coarsely grated Parmesan cheese

Peel potatoes and cut into cubes of about 1 inch. Heat oil in skillet and add potato cubes. Cook over medium heat, stirring and scraping occasionally, until potatoes have taken on color, about 10 minutes.

Add chicken stock; reduce heat, cover and simmer liquid for about 7 minutes longer, until potatoes are tender.

Grate cheese and sprinkle over potatoes. Cover and allow to sit over low heat another minute or two, until cheese melts. Season with freshly ground black pepper and serve.

Curried tomatoes and onion (2 SERVINGS)

1 small onion
1 small clove garlic
1½ teaspoons corn oil
1 pound tomatoes

1 teaspoon minced fresh ginger
½ teaspoon curry powder
Freshly ground black pepper
to taste

Chop onion, mince garlic and sauté in hot oil for about 3 minutes, until onion begins to soften. Coarsely chop tomatoes, mince ginger; add with remaining ingredients and cook over medium-high heat until tomatoes are soft and have released their juices, 5 to 7 minutes longer.

Scallops on a bed of red onions
Creamy tomato-cheese noodles
Steamed snow peas

MENU ANALYSIS SUMMARY

	NUTRIENTS PER SERVING		
	CALORIES	% FAT	SODIUM (MG)
Scallops on a bed of red onions	268	77	294
Creamy tomato-cheese noodles	453	16	97
Steamed snow peas	71	0	2
Totals for each individual/meal	792	35	393

Fiber per person: about 5½ grams

SHOPPING LIST

1½ pounds red onions

¾ pound bay or calico scallops

¾ pound snow peas

9 ounces spiral noodles

Small carton low-fat, no-salt-added cottage cheese (¾ cup)

Bunch scallions (3)

STAPLES

Olive oil

Sugar

Lemon

Black pepper

Unsalted butter

Garlic

Dry vermouth

Plain, low-fat yogurt

Tomato paste

Dry mustard

Caraway seeds

GAME PLAN

Bring noodle water to boil.

Slice and cook onions.

Prepare snow peas.

Prepare scallops and crush garlic.

Boil water for snow peas.

Add water and sugar to onions.

Make sauce for noodles.

Cook noodles.

Steam snow peas.

Add lemon juice and pepper to onions.

Cook scallops.

Combine noodles and sauce.

Scallops on a bed of red onions   (3 SERVINGS)

1½ pounds red onions
2 tablespoons olive oil
⅓ cup water
2 teaspoons sugar
2 teaspoons lemon juice
Freshly ground black pepper
to taste

¾ pound bay or calico scallops
1 tablespoon unsalted butter
1 medium clove garlic
2 tablespoons dry vermouth

Slice onions very thinly, using slicing blade of food processor, if desired. Sauté onions in hot oil over medium-high heat until onions soften, 10 to 12 minutes. Add water and sugar; cover and cook over low heat until water is evaporated, about 12 to 15 minutes longer. Sprinkle with lemon juice and pepper and keep warm over very low heat while scallops cook.

Wash and drain scallops. Heat butter; crush garlic. Add scallops and garlic to hot butter for 2 to 3 minutes, just long enough to cook scallops. Stir in vermouth; raise heat and cook quickly for 30 seconds. Spoon scallops over bed of red onions along with liquid.

114

Creamy tomato-cheese noodles (3 SERVINGS)

9 ounces spiral noodles

1 cup plain, low-fat yogurt

¾ cup low-fat, no-salt-added cottage cheese

3 tablespoons tomato paste

½ teaspoon dry mustard

1 large clove garlic

3 scallions

1½ teaspoons caraway seeds

Freshly ground black pepper to taste

Bring 3 quarts of water to boil in covered pot. Add noodles and cook according to package directions, until noodles are al dente, not soft.

In bowl of food processor combine yogurt, cottage cheese, tomato paste and mustard and blend until mixture is completely smooth. While machine is on, open top and add garlic, cut in three pieces. Continue blending.

Slice scallions and add with caraway seeds and pepper to sauce, stirring well. Serve over hot noodles.

Steamed snow peas (3 SERVINGS)

¾ pound snow peas

Bring water to boil in steamer.

Cut tips off snow peas and remove string. Wash. Add snow peas to steamer and cook for about 3 minutes, until snow peas take on a bright green color. Drain and serve.

Steamed fish with ginger
Scalloped potatoes
Tomato and scallion salad

A very low-fat meal, so that you might want to have this when you were having a breakfast or lunch that was higher in fat—butter on the morning English muffins, sandwich for lunch made with mayonnaise or salad with a lot of dressing. Or to increase the calories in the meal you could have a rich dessert.

MENU ANALYSIS SUMMARY

	NUTRIENTS PER SERVING		
	CALORIES	% FAT	SODIUM (MG)
Steamed fish with ginger	109	8	134
Scalloped potatoes	213	21	206
Tomato and scallion salad	80	36	7
Totals for each individual/meal	402	20	347

Fiber per person: a little over 4 grams

SHOPPING LIST

4 dried Chinese black mushrooms

1 bunch scallions (3)

¾ pound fillets of sole or flounder

1 pound tiny new potatoes

1 pound ripe tomatoes

1 ounce Parmesan (1 tablespoon)

Sesame oil (2 teaspoons)

STAPLES

Fresh ginger

Rice vinegar

Reduced-sodium soy sauce

Sugar

White pepper

Chicken broth

Unsalted butter

Flour

Rosemary

Thyme

Black pepper

Plain, low-fat yogurt

Soak mushrooms.

Cook potatoes.

Prepare tomato salad.

Prepare fish and fish topping.

Boil water in steamer.

Prepare cream sauce and cook.

Prepare mushrooms.

Cook fish.

Grate cheese and stir into cream sauce with yogurt.

Mix potatoes with cream sauce.

Steamed fish with ginger   (3 SERVINGS)

4 dried Chinese black mushrooms

2 scallions

3 thin slices fresh ginger, about the size of a quarter in diameter

¾ pound fillets of sole or flounder

¾ teaspoon rice vinegar

1 teaspoon reduced-sodium soy sauce

⅛ teaspoon sugar

White pepper to taste

Soak mushrooms in hot water to cover for 20 minutes.

Slice scallions thinly.

Cut ginger into fine julienne strips.

Slice fillets lengthwise in half. Arrange either on aluminum foil package in top of steamer or in shallow dish that fits in steamer.

Combine scallions, ginger, vinegar, soy sauce, sugar and white pepper and spoon over fillets.

When mushrooms have soaked, remove from water, cut off stems and discard. Slice mushrooms into thin strips and sprinkle over fish.

Place in steamer over boiling water and steam 5 or 6 minutes, until cooked.

Scalloped potatoes

1 pound tiny new potatoes
1 tablespoon unsalted butter
1 tablespoon flour
¾ cup plus 2 tablespoons chicken broth or stock
¼ teaspoon dried rosemary

¼ teaspoon dried thyme
Freshly ground black pepper to taste
1 tablespoon coarsely grated Parmesan cheese
½ cup plain, low-fat yogurt

Scrub potatoes but do not peel and cook in water to cover in covered pot until potatoes are just tender, about 20 minutes. Remove from heat and place in serving bowl.

Melt butter in small saucepan; stir in flour and cook about 1 minute, stirring. Remove from heat and stir in stock with rosemary, thyme and pepper. Return to heat and continue cooking until mixture thickens. Grate cheese. Remove from heat, stir in yogurt and cheese.

Cut potatoes in halves or quarters, depending on size, and stir sauce in, mixing well.

NOTE TO COOK: The potatoes are best when they are mashed up with the sauce.

Tomato and scallion salad

2 teaspoons sesame oil
4 teaspoons rice vinegar
1 pound ripe tomatoes

1 large scallion
Freshly ground black pepper to taste

Beat oil with vinegar in bowl large enough to hold tomatoes.
Cut tomatoes into small chunks.
Slice scallion into thin rings.
Add tomatoes and scallion to dressing and stir well. Season with freshly ground black pepper and refrigerate until serving time.

Scallops and fresh coriander
"Creamed" yellow squash
Warm potatoes vinaigrette

This is a rich meal, one of those days you need to make sure that breakfast and lunch are low-fat meals: stay away from salad dressings, oil, butter, whole milk products and cheeses to reduce the average fat intake to 35 percent or less. Have a toasted bagel and low-fat yogurt for breakfast, vegetable soup or fruit plate for lunch.

MENU ANALYSIS SUMMARY

	NUTRIENTS PER SERVING		
	CALORIES	% FAT	SODIUM (MG)
Scallops and fresh coriander	326	50	370
"Creamed" yellow squash	107	59	139
Warm potatoes vinaigrette	333	37	13
1 whole-grain roll	125	7	125
Totals for each individual/meal	891	40	647

Fiber per person: about 11 grams

SHOPPING LIST

¾ pound bay or sea scallops
  White wine (¼ cup)
  Bunch fresh coriander (cilantro or Chinese parsley) (1½ tablespoons)
  Bunch fresh parsley (2 tablespoons)
  Bunch scallions (4 whole plus 2 tablespoons)

1¼ pound summer squash
  Bunch fresh basil (¼ cup) (optional)
1 pound tiny new potatoes
  Whole-grain roll
2 ounces Parmesan cheese (3 tablespoons)

STAPLES

Flour
Black pepper
Peanut oil
Butter
Dried basil

Plain, low-fat yogurt
Cornstarch
Olive oil
White wine vinegar
Oregano

Cook potatoes.

Cut squash; chop fresh basil.

Flour scallops.

Chop coriander and parsley; slice scallions.

Grate cheese.

Mix yogurt and cornstarch.

Chop scallions and make dressing for potatoes.

Cook squash and basil.

Cook scallops.

Deglaze pan and set aside.

Mix potatoes with dressing.

Add yogurt to squash; add cheese and pepper.

Finish cooking scallops.

Scallops and fresh coriander   (3 SERVINGS)

2 to 3 tablespoons flour

Freshly ground black pepper to taste

¾ pound bay scallops or ¾ pound sea scallops cut in quarters, washed, drained and dried thoroughly

1½ tablespoons chopped fresh coriander leaves (cilantro or Chinese parsley)

2 tablespoons chopped fresh parsley

2 tablespoons thinly sliced scallions

1 tablespoon peanut oil

2 tablespoons unsalted butter, cut into small pieces

¼ cup dry white wine

Mix flour and pepper together in plate or a bowl. Dredge scallops very lightly in the mixture and set aside.

Chop coriander and parsley; slice scallions.

Heat oil and 1 tablespoon butter in large skillet. Add scallops and sauté for 2 minutes over medium-high heat, stirring frequently. Remove from pan and pour off excess fat.

Add the wine to pan and deglaze by scraping up the browned bits on the bottom with a wooden spoon. Bring to a boil and whisk in the remaining butter, one small piece at a time. Return the scallops to the pan over medium-high heat and add the coriander, parsley and scallions. Cook 1 to 2 minutes longer or just until scallops are heated through. (Do not overcook or sauce will become gluey.) Adjust seasonings.

"Creamed" yellow squash (3 SERVINGS)

1¼ pounds yellow summer squash

¼ cup freshly chopped fresh basil or 2 teaspoons dried basil

1 tablespoon unsalted butter

½ teaspoon cornstarch

¼ cup plain, low-fat yogurt

3 tablespoons coarsely grated Parmesan cheese

Freshly ground black pepper to taste

Cut ends off squash after scrubbing. Cut in half horizontally, then slice thinly to make long sticks. Chop fresh basil.

Heat butter in 10-inch skillet. Add squash and basil. Cook over medium-high heat, stirring frequently, for about 5 minutes, until squash begins to soften.

Blend cornstarch with yogurt and stir into squash, mixing to heat through. Grate cheese and sprinkle over squash with pepper.

Warm potatoes vinaigrette (3 SERVINGS)

10 small boiling potatoes, about 1 pound

2 tablespoons olive oil

4 tablespoons white wine vinegar

4 scallions

½ teaspoon dried oregano

Freshly ground black pepper to taste

Scrub potatoes, leaving skins on. Boil until tender, about 20 minutes.

Beat oil with vinegar. Mince scallions and add with oregano to oil and vinegar. Season with pepper. Place cooked potatoes in serving bowl; cut into halves or quarters, depending on size. Pour over dressing and stir to mix well.

Flounder in orange sauce with pine nuts
Warm potatoes and green bean salad

Add a piece of fruit for dessert, increasing the calorie count by 50 to 75 calories, reducing the percentage of fat to 35 percent.

MENU ANALYSIS SUMMARY

	NUTRIENTS PER SERVING		
	CALORIES	% FAT	SODIUM (MG)
Flounder in orange sauce with pine nuts	*223–334*	*29*	*72–108*
Warm potatoes and green bean salad	*363*	*45*	*21*
Totals for each individual/meal	*586–697*	*37*	*93–129*

Fiber per person: almost 7 grams

SHOPPING LIST

½ to ⅔ pound flounder fillet

1 ounce pine nuts (2 tablespoons)

Small can frozen orange juice concentrate (2 tablespoons)

Bunch fresh parsley (1 tablespoon)

8 to 10 ounces tiny new potatoes

½ pound fresh green beans

Bunch scallions (¼ cup)

Bunch fresh dill (3 tablespoons)

STAPLES

Olive oil

Raisins

Lemon

Red wine vinegar

Dried mustard

Black pepper

GAME PLAN

Scrub and cook potatoes.

Wash and cut tips off green beans.

Turn on broiler.

Make fish sauce.

Oil fish and place on broiler pan.

Make dressing for beans and potatoes.

Add beans to potato water.

Broil fish.

Drain beans and potatoes and mix with dressing.

Reheat fish sauce; chop and add parsley and spoon over fish.

Flounder in orange sauce with pine nuts　　　　(2 SERVINGS)

½ to ⅔ pound flounder fillet

1 tablespoon olive oil plus a few drops

2 tablespoons raisins

2 tablespoons pine nuts

2 tablespoons orange juice concentrate

1 teaspoon lemon juice

1 teaspoon water

1 tablespoon chopped fresh parsley

Turn on broiler. Cut the fillet in half and place on broiler pan (use toaster oven if you have one). Rub with a few drops oil.

Heat 1 tablespoon oil in small skillet.

Sauté raisins and pine nuts over medium heat until pine nuts color, about 2 or 3 minutes. Stir in orange juice concentrate, lemon juice and water. Remove from heat.

Broil fish about 2 inches from source of heat about 7 or 8 minutes, just until fish flakes easily with fork. Don't overcook.

Reheat sauce; chop parsley and add. Spoon over fillets on individual plates.

Warm potatoes and green bean salad

8 to 10 ounces tiny new potatoes
½ pound green beans
2½ tablespoons red wine vinegar
2½ tablespoons olive oil
½ teaspoon dried mustard

¼ cup sliced scallions
3 tablespoons snipped fresh dill
Freshly ground black pepper to taste

Scrub potatoes. Do not peel. Cook in enough water to cover potatoes and the green beans, which will be added eventually. Cook potatoes about 20 minutes, until tender.

Meanwhile, wash green beans and cut off tips. When potatoes have cooked about 15 minutes, add green beans to pot and cook until green beans are done, 5 to 7 minutes. They should be crisp-tender. If they are done before potatoes, remove green beans and continue cooking potatoes. Drain.

While vegetables are cooking, combine vinegar, oil and mustard in a serving bowl large enough to hold vegetables. Whisk the dressing to blend.

Cut scallions into thin rings. Cut dill into small pieces. Add scallions and dill to dressing. When vegetables are cooked, add to bowl, cutting beans in half and potatoes into quarters. Mix thoroughly with dressing and season with pepper. Serve warm.

Salmon and olive sauce
Linguine
Tomatoes, basil and goat cheese

You can further lower fat by using a less fatty fish such as flounder.

MENU ANALYSIS SUMMARY

	NUTRIENTS PER SERVING		
	CALORIES	% FAT	SODIUM (MG)
Salmon and olive sauce	349	62	491
Linguine	210	0	2
Tomatoes, basil and goat cheese	123	37	95
Totals for each individual/meal	682	39	588

Fiber per person: about 4½ grams

SHOPPING LIST

½ pound salmon fillet

1 to 2 ounces olives packed in brine
(2 tablespoons)

4 ounces linguine

1 pound tomatoes

10 fresh basil leaves

1 ounce goat cheese (2 tablespoons)

STAPLES

Olive oil

Onion

Garlic

Oregano

Black pepper

GAME PLAN

Boil water for pasta.

Broil fish.

Cook pasta.

Prepare onion, garlic and olives.

Sauté sauce ingredients.

Start salad.

Mix cooked fish and sauce
ingredients.

Drain pasta and mix with sauce.

Finish salad.

Salmon and olive linguine (2 SERVINGS)

½ pound pink salmon fillet, skinned

1 tablespoon olive oil

1 medium onion

1 clove garlic

2 tablespoons chopped Greek or other olives packed in brine

1 teaspoon dried oregano leaves

Freshly ground black pepper to taste

Broil fish in toaster oven if you have one or in broiler of oven, 5 to 7 minutes, depending on thickness of fish.

Chop onion medium fine and mince garlic or put through press. Sauté onion and garlic in hot oil until onion is soft. Chop olives.

Add oregano and olives and stir; cook 2 minutes over low heat.

When salmon is cooked, cut into small pieces and add to onion. Reheat and serve mixed with pasta.

Serve with freshly ground black pepper.

Linguine (2 SERVINGS)

4 ounces linguine

Water

Bring 2 quarts water to boil in covered pot. Add linguine and cook uncovered, until linguine is al dente, about 12 to 15 minutes.

Drain and return to pot. Allow a little of the water to remain with the linguine. Toss with salmon and olive sauce.

Tomatoes, basil and goat cheese (2 SERVINGS)

2 ripe tomatoes, about 1 pound

10 fresh basil leaves

2 tablespoons fresh goat cheese such as Boucheron or Montrachet

Freshly ground black pepper to taste

Wash, core and slice tomatoes thickly. Arrange on plate with basil leaves between each slice. Crumble goat cheese on top of each plate and sprinkle with freshly ground black pepper.

Moroccan lamb sausage (F)
Minted bulgur with peas
Braised brussels sprouts

Don't buy already ground lamb: It has too much fat in it. If you don't want to grind the lamb at home, pick out a lean piece and have the butcher grind it for you.

MENU ANALYSIS SUMMARY

	NUTRIENTS PER SERVING		
	CALORIES	% FAT	SODIUM (MG)
Moroccan lamb sausage	304	35	132
Minted bulgur	199	9	48
with almonds	244	22	49
Braised brussels sprouts	111	4	21
Totals for each individual/meal	614	25	201
with almonds	659	29	202

Fiber per person: 8 grams
Fiber per person (with almonds): 9 grams

GAME PLAN

Defrost frozen peas, if used.

Soak bulgur.

Turn on broiler.

Boil butter and broth.

Prepare and cook scallions and brussels sprouts.

Broil lamb.

Toast almonds, if used.

Shell fresh peas, if used, and cook.

Finish preparing bulgur.

Moroccan lamb sausage (F)   (4 SERVINGS)

1 pound lean lamb

6 tablespoons chopped fresh parsley

6 tablespoons chopped onion

½ teaspoon dried marjoram

½ teaspoon cumin powder

½ teaspoon ground coriander seed

½ teaspoon dried oregano

¼ teaspoon cayenne

Freshly ground black pepper to taste

Grind lamb and add parsley and onion; mix well. Add remaining ingredients and mix thoroughly; grind again.

Divide into four portions and, with moist hands, shape into sausages 1½ to 2 inches thick and about 4½ inches long. Freeze.

To serve, defrost and broil or barbecue 4 inches from source of heat until brown, about 10 minutes for lamb pink inside, about 15 minutes for well done.

Minted bulgur with peas

1 cup bulgur

2 cups fresh peas or 1 (10-ounce) package frozen peas

½ cup toasted sliced almonds (optional)

1 tablespoon chopped fresh basil

¼ cup minced fresh parsley

4 tablespoons minced fresh mint

3 scallions, sliced

1 tablespoon freshly squeezed lemon juice

Freshly ground black pepper to taste

1 cup plain, low-fat yogurt

Cover bulgur with boiling water and allow to stand for 25 minutes. Drain thoroughly, squeezing out additional water with hands.

Cook fresh peas in boiling water for 1 minute; drain. Or defrost frozen peas but do not cook. Combine peas with bulgur and remaining ingredients except for yogurt. Then stir in yogurt to coat thoroughly.

Braised brussels sprouts

2 tablespoons unsalted butter

½ cup chicken broth or stock

1 medium onion, minced

2 pints brussels sprouts, washed and trimmed

Freshly ground black pepper to taste

Bring butter and broth to boil. Add onion and brussels sprouts; reduce heat; cover and simmer 15 to 20 minutes, until tender. Toss brussels sprouts once or twice during cooking.

Season with pepper.

Broiled lamb chops with apricots (F)
Snow peas and red pepper salad
Greek-style rice

If you want to add more calories without adding more fat to the meal, consider a bottle of beer for 150 or a glass of wine for about 100.

MENU ANALYSIS SUMMARY

	NUTRIENTS PER SERVING		
	CALORIES	% FAT	SODIUM (MG)
Broiled lamb chops with apricots	174	21	50
Snow peas and red pepper salad	188	72	9
Greek-style rice	304	6	42
Totals for each individual/meal	666	28	101

Fiber per person: a little over 5½ grams

GAME PLAN

Preheat broiler.

Chop onion and cook with rice.

Prepare snow peas and red pepper.

Broil chops.

Toast sesame seeds and prepare garlic.

Prepare spinach; squeeze lemon juice.

Turn chops.

Make salad dressing; add snow peas and red pepper.

Add spinach, lemon juice and pepper to cooked rice.

Sprinkle sesame seeds on salad.

Broiled lamb chops with apricots (F)   (2 SERVINGS)

8 small dried apricot halves

1 tablespoon finely chopped onion

2 double-rib lamb chops (or loin), with pocket cut between bones, completely trimmed of fat

½ teaspoon dried rosemary

½ teaspoon dried thyme

½ teaspoon grated lemon peel

Freshly ground black pepper to taste

Divide apricots and onion in half and insert the apricots and onion into each pocket of chops.

Press the herbs, lemon peel and pepper on both sides of each chop.

Freeze.

To serve, defrost. Heat broiler (of toaster oven if you have one) and place lightly greased broiler rack 5 inches from source of heat. After broiler is heated, broil chops about 7 to 10 minutes on each side, until crusty but still pink inside.

Snow peas and red pepper salad (2 SERVINGS)

¼ pound snow peas
1 tablespoon sesame seeds
1 small clove garlic, pressed
1 tablespoon corn oil
1 teaspoon sesame oil

1 tablespoon white wine vinegar
1 large red pepper, washed, cored, seeded and cut into julienne strips
Freshly ground black pepper

Wash peas; remove tips, string and cut in half.

While peas are being prepared, toast sesame seeds until golden.

In serving bowl place garlic and corn and sesame oils and beat in vinegar. Add snow peas and red pepper. Season with pepper and stir to blend well.

Just before serving, stir in toasted sesame seeds.

Greek-style rice (2 SERVINGS)

¾ cup brown rice
1½ cups water
3 tablespoons finely chopped onion

¼ pound fresh spinach
4 teaspoons lemon juice
Freshly ground black pepper to taste

Soak rice in water for at least 2 hours or overnight. Add onion to rice and soaking water and cook 17 to 20 minutes, until rice is tender and water has been absorbed.

Wash spinach and drain; tear into small pieces. When rice is ready, stir in spinach and lemon juice and season with pepper. Stir until spinach begins to wilt.

Orange lamb chops (F)
Broiled eggplant
Potato and celery root puree

A low-fat, low-calorie meal, good for a day when you have a high-fat lunch or breakfast.

MENU ANALYSIS SUMMARY

	NUTRIENTS PER SERVING		
	CALORIES	% FAT	SODIUM (MG)
Orange lamb chops	169	27	43
Broiled eggplant	35	0	2
Potato and celery root puree	165	5	182
Totals for each individual/meal	369	15	227

Fiber per person: a little over 6 grams

GAME PLAN

Prepare potatoes, celery root and onion and steam.

Turn on broiler.

Slice onion and place in pot with marinade.

Prepare eggplant.

Broil chops.

Cook onion in marinade.

Broil eggplant.

Turn chops.

Chop scallions.

Turn eggplant.

Puree vegetables and season.

Pour marinade over chops.

Orange lamb chops (F)   (4 SERVINGS)

4 double-thick rib lamb chops or 4 sirloin steak lamb chops,* trimmed of all external fat

2 teaspoons dried rosemary

1 teaspoon dried thyme

¼ cup orange juice

1 tablespoon Worcestershire sauce

¼ cup white wine

1 large onion, thinly sliced

* Four shoulder chops may be substituted.

Rub herbs into both sides of chops.

Arrange chops in single layer in shallow pan.

Combine orange juice with Worcestershire sauce and wine. Pour over chops. Freeze chops in portions suitable for your family.

To serve, defrost chops, drain off marinade and place in small pot with thinly sliced onion, pulled into rings. Place chops in broiler pan and place broil pan about 4 inches from source of heat, depending on thickness of chops. Broil chops: about 12 minutes total for thin chops; about 15 minutes total for double-rib chops, turning once.

Meanwhile, cook the onions with marinade until onions are limp. Pour mixture over chops and serve.

Broiled eggplant (4 SERVINGS)

1½ pounds eggplant

Wash eggplant and cut off ends. Slice eggplant into ½-inch-thick slices and place in single layer on broiler pan. Add eggplant to chops about 4 inches from source of heat, and broil 3 to 4 minutes on each side. Watch carefully so slices do not burn, but they should brown.

NOTE: If desired, eggplant may be peeled.

Potato and celery root puree (4 SERVINGS)

1 pound large new potatoes, quartered, but not peeled

2 pounds celery root, peeled and quartered

1 large onion, quartered

Freshly ground black pepper to taste

4 scallions, chopped

Milk (optional)

Place potatoes, celery root and onion in steamer and steam until tender, 20 to 25 minutes.

Transfer to food processor and puree. Season with freshly ground pepper and serve sprinkled with chopped scallions.

Depending on the water content of the vegetables, a little milk may be necessary to thin the puree.

The potato skins may be peeled after cooking, if desired, for a whiter-looking puree, but it is not necessary.

Spicy lamb in pocket bread (F)
Butternut squash with raisins
Greens and lemon vinaigrette

NOTE: Add bread and fruit for dessert to increase calories without increasing fat.

MENU ANALYSIS SUMMARY

	NUTRIENTS PER SERVING		
	CALORIES	% FAT	SODIUM (MG)
Spicy lamb in pocket bread	306	14	203
Butternut squash with raisins	119	23	40
Greens and lemon vinaigrette	79	80	21
Totals for each individual/meal	504	26	264

Fiber per person: a little over 9 grams

GAME PLAN

Prepare squash and cook.

Wash and dry lettuce.

Heat lamb.

Prepare salad dressing and mix with lettuce.

Toast pitas.

Drain squash, puree and season.

Spicy lamb in pocket bread (F)   (4 SERVINGS)

1¼ pounds ground lamb

1 cup chopped onion

1 clove garlic, minced or put through press

28-ounce can no-salt-added plum tomatoes, drained

¾ teaspoon ground cumin

⅛ teaspoon cayenne

Freshly ground black pepper to taste

4 whole-wheat pitas

Brown lamb in its own fat and cook until it releases most of its fat. Pour off as much fat as possible and add the onion and garlic. Sauté until onion is soft. Crush tomatoes with hand and add to lamb with cumin and cayenne. Season to taste with black pepper and freeze, in portions suitable for your family's use.

To serve, defrost and heat through. Toast pitas and cut off about ¼ inch of the tops. Stuff meat into breads and serve.

Meat can be reheated from frozen state over very low heat; it must be done very slowly so it does not burn or dry out.

Butternut squash with raisins   (4 SERVINGS)

2 pounds butternut squash
1 tablespoon unsalted butter
1 tablespoon Worcestershire
  sauce

2 tablespoons raisins

Peel squash and seed. Cut into small pieces. Cover with water in saucepan and cook over high heat, about 10 minutes, until squash is tender. Drain well and either mash or put through food processor with butter and Worcestershire. Stir in raisins.

Greens and lemon vinaigrette   (4 SERVINGS)

2 scallions, finely chopped
3 tablespoons olive oil
1½ tablespoons lemon juice
⅓ teaspoon Dijon mustard
¼ teaspoon dried basil
  Freshly ground black pepper
  to taste

8 ounces soft leaf lettuce, torn
  into bite-size pieces

Combine scallions, oil, lemon juice, mustard, basil and pepper and beat well. Add the lettuce and toss to coat leaves.

Ginger pork chops with apples and prunes (F)
New potatoes
Herbed cucumbers
Fruit ice

This is a day to watch your fat intake. Make your other two meals low in fat: cereal, toasted muffin with jelly, no butter. For lunch: soup, salad with yogurt dressing, plain broiled fish and steamed vegetables.

MENU ANALYSIS SUMMARY

	NUTRIENTS PER SERVING		
	CALORIES	% FAT	SODIUM (MG)
Ginger pork chops with apples and prunes	*626*	*35*	*126*
New potatoes	*126*	*0*	*5*
Herbed cucumbers	*131*	*82*	*16*
Fruit ice	*70*	*0*	*0*
Totals for each individual/meal	*953*	*35*	*147*

Fiber per person: about 8 grams

GAME PLAN

Prepare potatoes and cook.
Prepare cucumbers.
Chop chives and parsley.
Heat chops.

Sauté cucumbers with chives in butter.
Sprinkle cucumbers with parsley.

Ginger pork chops with apples and prunes (F) (4 SERVINGS)

8 pitted prunes, cut in half
¼ cup brandy
4 thick center-cut pork chops, trimmed completely of fat
Freshly ground black pepper to taste
2 tablespoons corn oil
2 garlic cloves, minced

Zest of ½ lemon, coarsely grated
2 slices fresh ginger, minced
1 large apple, cored and thickly sliced
1 cup apple juice
1 cup plain, low-fat yogurt mixed with 1 tablespoon cornstarch

Put prunes in bowl with brandy while you prepare rest of ingredients.

Season chops with pepper. Heat oil in skillet large enough to hold the chops. Sauté chops with the lemon zest, garlic and ginger in the hot oil until chops are browned on both sides. Add apples, prunes, brandy and apple juice. Cover and cook until chops are tender, 20 to 30 minutes.

Stir yogurt with cornstarch and mix into chops. Stir to mix well with sauce; reduce heat and cook just until sauce thickens a bit and is heated through.

Freeze, in portions suitable for your family's use. To serve, defrost and reheat slowly in covered pan.

NOTE TO COOK: If you wish to use thin chops, they will cook in 20 minutes total cooking time.

New Potatoes   (4 SERVINGS)

20 ounces tiny new potatoes   Water

Scrub potatoes, but do not peel. Place in pot with water to cover. Bring to boil, covered, and boil 15 to 20 minutes, depending on size of potatoes, until tender. Drain and serve with sauce from pork chops.

Herbed cucumbers   (4 SERVINGS)

2 medium regular cucumbers or   2 tablespoons chopped fresh
   4 small Kirby cucumbers   parsley
2 tablespoons unsalted butter
1 to 2 tablespoons chopped fresh
   chives

If cucumbers are waxed, peel them. Otherwise wash and leave peel on. Cut off the ends and slice thinly.

Heat butter in skillet. Sauté cucumbers in hot butter with chives until cucumbers are limp, 5 to 7 minutes. Sprinkle with parsley and serve.

Texas pot roast (F)
Noodles, cheese and yogurt
Savory broccoli and onions

This is a day to treat yourself to some butter with your bread, even a rich dessert.

MENU ANALYSIS SUMMARY

	NUTRIENTS PER SERVING		
	CALORIES	% FAT	SODIUM (MG)
Texas pot roast	232	16	76
Noodles, cheese and yogurt	236	15	86
Savory broccoli and onions	92	9	44
Totals for each individual/meal	560	14	206

Fiber per person: about 3½ grams

GAME PLAN

Boil water in covered pot for pasta.

Prepare mushrooms and steam.

Prepare broccoli and onions.

Cook pasta.

Heat pot roast.

Heat chicken broth and cook broccoli and onions. Season.

Mince parsley.

Shred cheese and combine with yogurt and mushrooms.

Drain pasta and add to cheese-yogurt mixture. Season.

Texas pot roast (F)   (4 SERVINGS)

1 pound lean bottom round beef roast trimmed of all external fat

1 large onion, coarsely chopped

1 clove garlic, minced

½ teaspoon ground coriander seeds

¾ teaspoon ground cumin seeds

6-ounce can no-salt-added tomato paste, minus 2 tablespoons

¾ cup water

⅔ of 3-ounce can chopped green chiles

Freshly ground black pepper to taste

140

Brown meat on all sides in hot deep pot in its own fat. Add onion and garlic and cook until onion is soft, about 3 minutes, stirring occasionally. Stir in coriander, cumin, tomato paste, water, chiles and pepper. Bring to boil; reduce heat, cover and simmer until meat is tender, about 2 to 2½ hours.

Slice thinly and freeze in portions suitable for your family, covered with sauce.

To serve, defrost and reheat slowly in sauce.

Noodles, cheese and yogurt (4 SERVINGS)

¾ pound whole-wheat pasta shells (3 cups)

¾ pound fresh mushrooms, sliced

2 tablespoons dry vermouth

½ cup plus 2 tablespoons plain, low-fat yogurt

4 tablespoons coarsely shredded sharp cheddar cheese

¼ cup minced parsley

Freshly ground black pepper to taste

Cook pasta according to label directions. Steam mushroom slices in vermouth for about 3 minutes, until they are soft.

Combine yogurt and cheese in serving bowl. Stir in drained mushrooms and then cooked pasta. Mix well. Sprinkle with parsley and pepper.

Savory broccoli and onions (4 SERVINGS)

8 stalks broccoli

1½ cups chicken broth or stock

2 medium onions (about 1 cup), chopped

Freshly ground black pepper to taste

Trim tough ends off broccoli; wash and cut remaining stems into ¼-inch-thick slices. Separate florets into bite-size pieces. Heat broth in saucepan; add broccoli and onions; season with pepper and cover. Lower heat; simmer until broccoli is tender-crisp, about 10 minutes.

Hungarian-style steak (F)
Noodles
Zucchini bundles

Using lean cuts of meat it is possible to have beef in the diet and still keep both the fat and calories low . . . so long as you keep the portions small.

MENU ANALYSIS SUMMARY

	NUTRIENTS PER SERVING		
	CALORIES	% FAT	SODIUM (MG)
Hungarian-style steak	244	15	34
Noodles	236–295	0	2–3
Zucchini bundles	140	71	2
Totals for each individual/meal	620–679	24–26	38–39

Fiber per person: about 4 grams

GAME PLAN

Boil water in covered pot for noodles.

Prepare zucchini for salad.

Prepare dressing.

Heat steak.

Cook noodles.

Finish salad.

Hungarian-style steak (F)

(4 SERVINGS)

1 pound bottom round roast, trimmed of all fat and cut into 1-inch cubes

2 medium onions, chopped

1 large clove garlic, minced

1 teaspoon sweet Hungarian paprika

¼ teaspoon caraway seeds

2 tablespoons dry red wine

2 tablespoons red wine vinegar

2 tablespoons no-salt-added tomato paste

Freshly ground black pepper to taste

Water

In hot skillet, brown meat on all sides. Add onions and garlic and cook until onions soften. Add paprika and caraway seeds and stir. Stir in wine, vinegar, tomato paste and pepper. Add enough water to come about two thirds of the way up the sides of the meat. Bring to simmer and cook, covered, about 1 to 1¼ hours, stirring and turning meat occasionally until it is tender.

Freeze in portions suitable for your family's use. To serve, defrost and reheat gently.

Serve over noodles.

Thin noodles (4 SERVINGS)

8 to 10 ounces thin egg noodles
(2 to 2½ cups)

Cook noodles in 3 quarts boiling water according to package directions. Drain and serve with sauce from meat.

Zucchini bundles (4 SERVINGS)

3 zucchini, about 1 pound

3 tablespoons olive oil

1 tablespoon red wine vinegar

2 teaspoons fresh lime juice

1 teaspoon freshly grated or finely minced ginger

Freshly ground black pepper to taste

8 strips pimiento, about 3 inches long and ¼ inch wide

2 tablespoons finely minced fresh coriander (cilantro or Chinese parsley)

Trim the ends of the zucchini, scrub and either cut in half crosswise and then into matchstick pieces ⅛ inch thick or put through food processor using julienne blade.

Whisk the oil, vinegar, lime juice and ginger in serving bowl. Add zucchini and season with pepper to taste.

Arrange the zucchini in bundles on four small serving plates and lay the strips of pimiento across each one to resemble a ribbon.

Sprinkle with coriander and serve.

Broccoli with bean curd and pork
Noodles

A fruit ice for dessert will add about 100 calories, no fat or sodium and a refreshing way to end the meal.

MENU ANALYSIS SUMMARY

	NUTRIENTS PER SERVING		
	CALORIES	% FAT	SODIUM (MG)
Broccoli with bean curd and pork	378	43	186
Noodles	236	0	2
Totals for each individual/meal	614	30	188

Fiber per person: a little over 4½ grams

SHOPPING LIST

8 ounces firm bean curd

2 pounds broccoli

Hot chili-garlic paste (1 to 2 teaspoons)

4 ounces lean ground pork

Hoisin sauce (2 to 3 tablespoons)

4 ounces Chinese egg noodles or American pasta like capelletti

STAPLES

Corn oil

Garlic

Ginger

Chicken broth

Cornstarch

GAME PLAN

Boil water for noodles.

Prepare bean curd.

Prepare broccoli.

Mince garlic; shred ginger and cook in hot oil with chili paste.

Add bean curd, then pork, then broccoli.

Mix cornstarch with broth. Combine with hoisin; add to broccoli. Cover and cook.

Cook noodles in boiling water.

Drain noodles; serve broccoli–bean curd over noodles.

Broccoli with bean curd and pork

8 ounces bean curd*
2 pounds broccoli
1 tablespoon corn oil
2 large cloves garlic
2 teaspoons shredded fresh
ginger

1 to 2 teaspoons hot chili–garlic
paste*
4 ounces lean ground pork
2 teaspoons cornstarch
⅔ cup chicken broth or stock
2 to 3 tablespoons hoisin sauce*

Drain bean curd and press between paper towels to remove moisture. Slice into ¼-inch cubes.

Remove tough stems from broccoli (reserve for other use) and cut florets into small pieces.

Mince garlic; shred ginger.

Heat oil in wok or large skillet over very high heat. Add garlic, ginger and chili paste. Stir, and when mixture begins to color, reduce heat and add bean curd. Stir for 2 minutes, until bean curd begins to color. Add pork and cook until it loses its pink color, stirring. Add broccoli; stir for 2 minutes. Mix cornstarch with a little broth. Combine with remaining broth and hoisin; stir into broccoli. Cover; reduce heat and simmer 3 to 5 minutes, just until broccoli is crisp-tender.

Serve over noodles.

Chinese noodles

4 ounces Chinese egg noodles or
American very, very thin pasta,
like capelletti

Water

Bring 6 quarts to boil in covered pot. Add noodles and cook according to package directions. Drain well and serve on plate topped with broccoli–bean curd mixture.

* Try to buy firm rather than soft bean curd if it is available. Bean curd, hoisin and hot chili–garlic paste are available in Oriental grocery stores and elsewhere.

Stir-fried eggs with pork, noodles and coriander
Zucchini with vermouth
Brown rice
Fruit ice or beer

If you choose beer instead of fruit ice, use figures in parentheses.

MENU ANALYSIS SUMMARY

	NUTRIENTS PER SERVING		
	CALORIES	% FAT	SODIUM (MG)
Stir-fried eggs with pork, noodles and coriander	440	70	484
Zucchini with vermouth	53	0	trace
Brown rice	234	5	6
¾ cup fruit ice	100	0	0
(or beer)	(150)	0	(25)
Totals for each individual/meal	827	35	490+
	(877)	(33)	(515)

Fiber per person: almost 7 grams

SHOPPING LIST

1 ounce cellophane noodles

¼ pound lean pork, ground or minced

5 slices nitrite-free bacon

Bunch celery (1 stalk)

Bunch scallions (3)

Bunch fresh coriander (cilantro or Chinese parsley) (¼ cup)

6 small zucchini

Fruit ice or beer

STAPLES

Corn oil

Cornstarch

Reduced-sodium soy sauce

Sugar

Black pepper

Eggs

Onion

Dry vermouth

Thyme

Brown rice

Soak noodles.

Cook rice.

Scrub zucchini and trim.

Chop onion and sauté in vermouth.

Combine oil, cornstarch, soy, sugar, pepper and pork.

Add zucchini to onion with thyme.

Cut bacon, celery, scallions.

Add remaining vermouth to zucchini; cover and cook.

Drain noodles and cut.

Heat oil in wok; add celery and scallions and stir-fry.

Add pork mixture and bacon; stir-fry.

Drain off fat.

Add noodles.

Cover and cook.

Chop coriander.

Add eggs and coriander.

Season zucchini.

Stir-fried eggs with pork, noodles and coriander (3 SERVINGS)

1 ounce cellophane noodles

2 tablespoons corn oil

1 teaspoon cornstarch

2 teaspoons reduced-sodium soy sauce

¼ teaspoon sugar

Dash pepper

¼ pound lean pork, ground or minced

5 slices nitrite-free bacon

1 stalk celery

3 scallions

4 eggs, beaten lightly

4 egg whites, beaten lightly

¼ cup chopped fresh coriander (cilantro or Chinese parsley) leaves

Soak the noodles in a bowl of tap water for about 20 minutes. Drain, cut in quarters and set aside. Combine 1 tablespoon of the oil, cornstarch, soy sauce, sugar and pepper together in a bowl. Add the pork and mix well with wooden spoon or hands.

Cut the bacon crosswise into thin strips and set aside. Coarsely chop celery and scallions. Heat remaining oil in skillet or wok. Add celery and scallions and stir-fry until celery begins to soften. Add the pork and bacon and stir-fry until meats lose their pink color. Drain off fat. Stir in noodles. Cover and cook 2 minutes. Chop coriander; add with eggs. Stir and cook until eggs reach desired firmness.

Zucchini with vermouth

6 small zucchini, about 1¼
  pounds
1 large onion
6 tablespoons dry vermouth

1 teaspoon dried thyme
Freshly ground black pepper
to taste

Scrub zucchini. Chop onion coarsely. Sauté onion in 3 tablespoons of vermouth for 3 minutes. Add zucchini and thyme and cook 5 minutes.

Add remaining vermouth; cover and cook about 15 minutes longer, until zucchini is tender. Season with pepper.

Brown rice

1 cup brown rice

2 cups water

The night before or no less than 2 hours before serving, cover the rice with the water and allow to sit in cooking pot.

To serve, bring water and rice to boil; reduce heat and simmer rice in covered pot until tender and water has been absorbed, 17 to 20 minutes.

Beef with scallions
Orange rice
Asparagus

Offer a double serving of rice for big eater.

MENU ANALYSIS SUMMARY

	NUTRIENTS PER SERVING		
	CALORIES	% FAT	SODIUM (MG)
Beef with scallions	*425*	*57*	*245*
Orange rice	*201*	*4*	*4*
Asparagus	*39*	*0*	*3*
Totals for each individual/meal	*665*	*38*	*252*

Fiber per person: a little over 5 grams

SHOPPING LIST

½ pound skirt or flank steak
2 bunches scallions
Small can orange juice concentrate
(2 tablespoons)

1 orange
1 pound asparagus

STAPLES

Reduced-sodium soy sauce
Dry sherry
Corn oil

Garlic
Fresh ginger
Brown rice

Defrost ginger if frozen and run orange juice concentrate under hot water, if frozen.

Wash and remove tough ends from asparagus.

Slice flank steak; mix with soy sauce and sherry.

Heat water for steaming asparagus.

Mince ginger.

Cut up scallions.

Grate orange rind.

Heat oil to cook beef.

Cook asparagus.

Cook beef, ginger; press garlic through press into wok.

Stir orange juice concentrate and rind into rice and keep warm.

Remove beef from oil and put in serving dish.

Add oil and heat.

Remove asparagus from heat and remove cover.

Add scallions to hot oil and cook; mix with beef.

Beef with scallions

(2 SERVINGS)

½ pound well-trimmed skirt or flank steak

2 teaspoons reduced-sodium soy sauce

1 tablespoon dry sherry

3 tablespoons minced fresh ginger

2 bunches scallions

3 tablespoons corn oil

2 large cloves garlic

Slice flank steak on diagonal into slices less than ¼ inch thick. Mix with soy sauce and sherry.

Mince ginger.

Cut scallions into 1-inch pieces.

Heat 2 tablespoons oil in wok or heavy skillet. Add beef mixture and ginger, put garlic through press directly into pan and stir-fry about 3 minutes, until beef loses pink color. Remove and keep warm in serving dish. Add remaining tablespoon oil and heat. Stir-fry scallions for about 1 to 1½ minutes, until shiny. Mix with beef and serve.

Orange rice

½ cup brown rice

2 tablespoons undiluted orange
juice concentrate

½ teaspoon grated orange rind

Soak rice in 1 cup water overnight or for at least 2 hours.

Bring the water and rice to boil in uncovered pan. Reduce heat to simmer and cover. Cook rice about 17 to 20 minutes, until rice is tender and water has evaporated. Grate rind. Stir in orange juice concentrate and rind and serve.

Asparagus

1 pound asparagus

Bring water to boil in steamer.

Rinse asparagus and break off tough bottom stems.

Steam asparagus about 10 minutes, just until crisp-tender in covered steamer.

Cooperative Dinners

Menus and recipes for cooperative dinners

NOTE: In the list below, F indicates that the dish may be prepared ahead of time and frozen; R indicates that it may be prepared ahead of time and refrigerated for the number of days given.

SPRING DINNER FOR 12   165

Smoked trout mousse (R2)
Bratwurst and apple phyllo (F/R3)
Shrimp with feta (R1)
Asparagus with pecans
Spiced olive salad (R1)
Chocolate chocolate pie (F/R2)

SPRING–SUMMER DINNER FOR 12   170

Mushroom caviar (R2)
Zucchini pancakes (R1)
Cold Chinese noodle salad (R1)
Shaking beef cubes
Steamed asparagus
Red pepper puree (R1)
"Kugelhopf"
Almond crescents (F/R2)

SUMMER DINNER FOR 12   177

Smoked mozzarella and sun-dried tomatoes (R3)
Lecso with sausages (R1)
Cumin beef balls (R1)
Lentils and goat cheese salad (R2)
Buttermilk potato salad (R1)
Zabaglione semifreddo (F) *with strawberries*

SUMMER DINNER FOR 20

Sesame toasts (R7)
New Mexican cheese spread (R1)
Basil, chicken and potatoes (R1)
Black-eyed pea and ham salad (R2)
Marinated mushrooms and cherry tomatoes (R3)
Poppy seed dressing for summer fruits (R1)
Chocolate chunk cookies (R2)

FALL—WINTER DINNER FOR 16

Three cheese pie (R3)
Portuguese pork and clams (R2)
Soy-marinated skirt steaks
Carrots with coriander
Cold broccoli with yogurt-ginger dressing (dressing R2)
Tortilla de patata
Pears poached in red wine with basil (R1)
Tuiles (R2)

FALL, WINTER, SPRING DINNER FOR 30

Oven-fried potato peelings (sauce R2; potatoes R1)
Frittatas (F/R1)
Cold Oriental noodles (R4)
Middle Eastern chicken with bulgur (F/R2)
Hot cherry tomatoes vinaigrette (R1)
Mushroom and fennel salad with cheeses and bread (R1)
Mocha almond cakes (F/R1)

FALL—WINTER DINNER FOR 16 OR 18

Bon bon chicken (R1)
Cheddar-cumin toast (R7)
Transylvanian cabbage (R1)
Apple-barley pilaf (R1)
Orange and red onion salad
Carrie Lee's vermicelli (sauce R1)
Ginger cheesecake (R2)
Black and white cheesecake (R2)

FALL—WINTER HOLIDAY DINNER FOR 18

Oysters with saffron-ginger sauce (sauce R1)
Roast turkey with pine nut and rice stuffing (stuffing R1)
Carrot puree (R1)
Cauliflower puree (R1)
Spiked cranberry-orange relish (R7)
Apple and endive salad with grapefruit dressing (dressing R1)
Pumpkin cheesecake in nut crust (R1)
Chocolate-pecan-grapefruit tartes (R1)

SUMMER BRUNCH FOR 12

Potato cheese pancakes
Sausages
Amaretto applesauce (F/R3)
Sherley's peaches with ginger berry sauce (sauce R1)
Giant oatmeal spice cookies (R1)
Coffee, tea, wine
Screwdrivers, Mimosas

ALL SEASONS BRUNCH OR LIGHT SUPPER FOR 12

Baked stuffed papaya (R1)
Fruits and vegetables (R1) *with peanut sauce* (R3)
Baltimore cheese bread (R1)
Whole-wheat blueberry muffins (F/R1)
Benne seed cookies (F/R7)
Coffee, tea, wine
Bloody Marys, Mimosas

Introduction to
Cooperative Dinners

The idea for cooperative dinner parties came to me when I moved to New York in 1981. There seemed to be no way to entertain our friends when we went back to Washington on weekends because I had no time to cook when I got there. But food is my profession and I had never had a catered dish in my house.

My desire to see friends, however, overcame my reluctance to ask them to do the cooking, and they responded with such enthusiasm that I realized I had come upon a modern version of the old potluck dinners. In the last two and a half years, in addition to tasting some wonderful dishes that friends have brought, I have discovered that this style of entertaining appeals to all busy people. What's more, it's a better icebreaker than two martinis or playing party games. And when you are asking someone to bring just one dish, you can be sure he or she will give it his or her undivided attention and make it quite spectacular.

As I investigated cooperative dinners further, I found that the tradition hadn't died out with the end of the Depression. While it remains a more popular form of entertaining in small towns, the trend is catching on again in big cities. The revolution in the workplace that has taken half of all women in this country out of their kitchens has made full-scale entertaining at home unrealistic without outside help such as the services of a caterer.

But catering has two serious drawbacks: It's very expensive, and even when you can afford it, after a while the guests recognize the caterer by the food. The other alternative is taking guests out to dinner, but that's even more expensive than hiring a caterer.

As I began to talk about these cooperative dinners and wrote an article in the *New York Times* describing the first one I did, I discovered more and more people who participated in them: from Supreme Court Justice Sandra Day O'Connor, who gave them once a year when she was a judge in Arizona, to Betty Friedan, who does it during the summer, to Dinah Shore, to my own literary agent and her husband, Ann and Art Buchwald. And, of course the biggest cooperative party of them all, my colleague Craig Claiborne's sixty-second birthday, to which some of the country's very best cooks and chefs brought their specialties.

But many people still feel a certain reluctance to ask their guests to provide food. There seem to be a number of explanations for this, none of them fully satisfactory. For some women there is the need to prove that they can do it all—the superwoman syndrome: work full time, keep house, raise children and be the perfect hostess. Then there is the need to prove that the family can afford to entertain; a desire to show off skills and/or a feeling of guilt if it is necessary to call on someone else to help. But none of these is a legitimate excuse. People just need a push, like Roger and E. J. Mudd, who gave their first cooperative party July 4, 1982. E. J. admitted to me that she tried it for the first time because "I figured if you could do it, I could, too." And so can everyone else.

The idea is catching on. In its party column a couple of summers ago, the *Times* recounted a birthday party an architect had thrown for himself and three hundred friends. He invited them to cruise around Manhattan one summer evening. Here is how the reporter explained it: ". . . and with more than a dash of chutzpah you ask those best pals to bring the dinner, allocating a specific course of ethnic food to each guest."

According to the account, the architect's friends were "not only amenable to providing food but also thought it was a great idea." So great that "the pizza, meat pies, corned-beef sandwiches, quiche, cheese, fruit and tarts they carried aboard Monday night were being gobbled up even before the departure horn hooted for the cruise."

To make a cooperative dinner work smoothly, you have to follow Dinah Shore's advice. Otherwise you will end up as she says, "With seven macaroni dishes on the buffet table." The host, or hostess, has to be the organizer and menu planner, not leaving the choice entirely up to the guests.

Here are a few simple rules for making a cooperative dinner a memorable gustatory experience as well as a delightful evening.

1 Tell your guests what kind of food to bring—salad, main dish, dessert, etc.—taking care to match up people with their specialties. Of course you will get a beautifully coordinated menu if all your guests own copies of this book. Otherwise you can offer to provide them with recipes from one of the menus you choose from the book.

Have the noncooks bring the wine or a wonderful bread. (When I first started arranging the dinners before I had learned better, one summer a bachelor showed up with two loaves of Wonder bread and a pound of margarine!) And tell those who are bringing the hors d'oeuvres to be on time.

2 As you get further into your guest list, people will have less choice about what they can bring. Once you have one chicken dish, you need beef, seafood or vegetarian, not another chicken.

For a dinner party where there is just one of each course you must be sure all the dishes go well together. If a casserole is made with sour cream, you certainly don't want a salad with yogurt dressing.

3 If you are having a large party, with a lot of food, mixing works well. Chinese dishes can sit side by side happily with Italian and Greek.

4 When there are a number of dishes, each one does not have to feed the entire group. For example, if you are having twenty people and three main dishes, each one needs to serve about twelve. There are always leftovers, of course, but the guests usually swap, seldom returning home with what they brought. (My friend Barbara Eagleton always accuses me of keeping the leftovers so I won't have to cook during the week. We would certainly eat well, if I did. Too well.)

5 Know what your kitchen can handle. If you have one oven, you won't be able to bake three different dishes, each requiring a different temperature. And keep in mind how many pots you can fit on the top of your stove simultaneously.

Beware of too many dishes requiring a lot of last-minute work unless you have a lot of work space in your kitchen.

6 If you do not have the appropriate serving dish, ask the guest to bring one. Dishes that can be served from the containers in which they were cooked are the easiest to manage.

7 When the dishes are put out on the buffet table, put the names of those who made them next to them so everyone receives proper credit and those who want the recipe know whom to ask.

8 How many serving dishes the hostess or host provides depends on the household's stock. But hosts should be responsible for all the silver, china, glassware, table decorations, cloths, napkins, ice and after-dinner beverages. Whether or not they are also responsible for the wine, liquor and soft drinks is up to them or up to the number of noncooks. We always provide all the drinks, with extra bottles of wine coming from those who want to add to the party but can't cook. On occasion I also cook a dish or surprise everyone with a specialty from New York that hasn't made its way to Washington yet.

If you don't have paid help to serve and clean up, noncooks can also participate by serving or washing the dishes.

9 With so many people cooking or preparing food in the kitchen at the same time, someone still needs to coordinate the dinner; otherwise it won't make it to the table. That is usually the job of the hostess or host.

We have given about a dozen cooperative dinners over the last two years and they have all been very successful because of the camaraderie.

The mood is bound to be informal when people come directly into the kitchen instead of heading for the bar. Even people who don't know one another have a common interest from the start.

To help you get started, take a look at the different menus for twelve to thirty people that follow. They are geared to different kinds of parties at different times of year, including one for a holiday dinner and two for brunch. They are divided according to seasons.

The recipes included with each menu will feed the number of people specified as long as they are served with the other dishes on that menu. Should you take any of the dishes and use them individually you will find that some of them serve fewer. For example, there is the recipe for Basil,

Chicken and Potatoes, page 206, that calls for 8 cups of cubed chicken and serves twenty people. It serves twenty people because there is also a recipe for black-eyed peas and ham salad on the same menu. If you serve the chicken salad alone, it would serve twelve to fourteen. You will have to rely on your experience as a cook to judge how many people any given dish will serve on its own.

Each of the recipes also carries a symbol if it can be made ahead of time and frozen (F), or if it can be made ahead and refrigerated (R). The number following the R indicates how many days in advance it can be made and refrigerated. A few dishes must be made the same day they are to be served, but most of the preparation can be done in advance.

Each recipe includes advice on how to transport the dish to the party, along with directions for last-minute preparation once you get there.

This chapter can also be used if you are asked to bring a dish to a cooperative dinner or to collaborate on one with another person. The recipes are broken down into categories in the introductory table of contents with page references.

Sometimes another friend and I tackle a dinner together. Sherley Koteen and I have been making New Year's Eve dinners that way for the last twelve years in Washington, and since I moved to New York, Carole Lalli and I have done several charity dinners together. It's much more fun and certainly half the work doing it with another person.

And on those special occasions when I have felt particularly ambitious, I have done all the cooking myself. The birthday party menu for thirty is a replication of one I did in January 1983 for Carrie Lee Nelson's birthday. I did most of the cooking in New York and transported it all to Washington in insulated containers. But you don't have to go that far.

I hope these menus will inspire you to start entertaining again, because now you know it can be fun.

Smoked trout mousse
Bratwurst and apple phyllo

Shrimp with feta
Asparagus with pecans
Spiced olive salad

Chocolate chocolate pie

Cooking facilities needed: oven, top of stove   *Silverware needed: forks*

Shrimp with feta, a Greek dish, is splendid for a very special dinner party. This is the kind of dinner one person could do alone, if necessary.

Smoked trout mousse (R2)   (3 CUPS)

2 8-ounce smoked trout
2 tablespoons chopped scallions
   White pepper to taste
⅛ teaspoon nutmeg
2 teaspoons chopped fresh dill
1 package unflavored gelatin

1½ cups heavy cream
½ cup plain yogurt
   Additional chopped fresh dill for garnish
   Melba toast

Skin and bone trout and puree in food processor with scallions, pepper, nutmeg and dill.

Soften gelatin in cream; then heat gently to dissolve completely. Add cream and yogurt to trout mixture and process to combine and make smooth.

Pour into decorative 3-cup mold or ring mold. Refrigerate overnight.

To unmold, run knife around edge. Fill sink with hot water. Hold mold in sink *a few seconds*, shaking until the mousse has pulled away from sides of mold. Unmold on serving dish and surround with melba toast.

NOTE TO COOK: Carry to party in mold. Carry melba toasts in plastic bag, chopped dill in another plastic bag. Unmold, decorate and serve.

165

4 bratwurst sausages	½ teaspoon ground coriander seed
1 tablespoon unsalted butter	
2 medium Granny Smith, MacIntosh or other tart apples, peeled and finely chopped	2 teaspoons grated fresh ginger
	12 sheets phyllo, approximately
1 teaspoon lemon juice	½ pound melted unsalted butter

Remove the sausages from the casings and chop into very small dice. Sauté in 1 tablespoon butter, browning lightly. Add the chopped apples and sauté until apples soften slightly. Add the lemon juice, coriander and ginger and mix well.

Cut the phyllo lengthwise into 4 strips. Place on damp cloth and cover with damp cloth to prevent phyllo from drying out. Working with one or two strips at a time, brush with melted butter. Fold over about ¼ inch of the bottom edge. Add a spoonful of the filling at the bottom edge and fold over to form a triangle. The folding is done as if you were folding an American flag from point to point. Place seam side down on baking sheets. When all the triangles have been made, brush tops with melted butter. Bake at 400 degrees for 20 to 30 minutes, until the tops are brown.

Freeze or refrigerate if desired. To serve, defrost if desired or reheat from frozen state. Reheat room-temperature triangles at 350 degrees for 10 to 15 minutes. Reheat frozen triangles at 350 degrees for 20 minutes.

NOTE TO COOK: Carry to party either on baking sheet or in container, already defrosted if they were frozen. Bake and serve warm.

Try to buy phyllo that has never been frozen. It is easier to work with. If you can find handmade, it is the best of all.

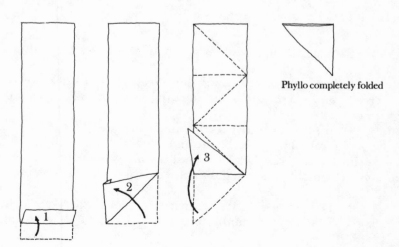

Phyllo completely folded

Shrimp with feta (RI) (12 SERVINGS)

SAUCE:

24 large ripe tomatoes or 16 cups chopped tomatoes

6 cups chopped onion

8 cloves garlic, minced

6 tablespoons olive oil

4 tablespoons fresh basil or 4 teaspoons dried basil

4 teaspoons ground cumin seed

2 teaspoons sugar

Freshly ground black pepper to taste

SHRIMP:

8 tablespoons unsalted butter

4 pounds shrimp, shelled

4 tablespoons ouzo (anise-flavored liqueur)

8 tablespoons cognac

1⅓ cups crumbled feta cheese

Chopped fresh parsley for garnish

Seed tomatoes and chop coarsely. Sauté onion and garlic in oil until onion softens but does not brown. Add tomatoes, basil, cumin, sugar and pepper. Cook, uncovered, about 30 minutes.

Melt butter in skillet large enough to hold shrimp and sauté shrimp just until it turns pink. Heat ouzo, flame and pour over shrimp. Repeat with cognac. Arrange shrimp and juice from pan in shallow casserole(s) and pour tomato sauce over. Top with feta and refrigerate, if desired.

To serve, remove from refrigerator 30 minutes before baking. Bake at 375 degrees 13 to 15 minutes, until mixture is hot and bubbly, but do not let shrimp overcook. Sprinkle with parsley.

NOTE TO COOK: Prepare dish and arrange in bake-and-serve casseroles. Cover with foil and bring to party. Bake and sprinkle with parsley.

Asparagus with pecans (12 SERVINGS)

6 pounds asparagus, trimmed and cooked until crisp-tender

6 tablespoons unsalted butter

1½ cups pecan pieces, toasted

Freshly ground black pepper and salt to taste

Place asparagus in shallow baking dish that has been greased with some of the butter. Dot asparagus with butter and sprinkle with pecans. Season to taste and bake at 350 degrees about 10 minutes, just until heated through.

NOTE TO COOK: Cook asparagus at home, early in the day if desired, but do not refrigerate. Carry to party in baking dish dotted with butter, sprinkled with pecans and seasoned. Bake and serve.

167

Spiced olive salad (R1)

2 cups brown or white rice

32 Greek olives, pitted

8 medium oranges, peeled and sectioned

2 cups sliced celery

¼ cup sliced scallions

6 tablespoons good-quality olive oil

4 tablespoons red wine vinegar

2 teaspoons ground coriander seed

¼ teaspoon cayenne

1 cup pine nuts, toasted

Cook rice and rinse with cold water; drain.

In serving bowl toss rice with olives, oranges, celery and scallions. In smaller bowl whisk together oil, vinegar, coriander and cayenne. Pour dressing over rice mixture and refrigerate for several hours or overnight. To serve, toss in pine nuts.

NOTE TO COOK: Carry dressed salad to party either in serving bowl wrapped tightly with plastic or in storage container. Carry pine nuts, already toasted, separately. At party arrange salad and add pine nuts just before serving.

Chocolate chocolate pie (F/R2)

Rich is hardly the word for this pie, which has a mousselike filling and a chocolate nut crust.

FILLING:

12 eggs, separated	3 ounces semisweet chocolate
1½ cups plus 3 tablespoons sugar	1 cup plus 2 tablespoons unsalted butter, softened
2 teaspoons vanilla extract	
¾ cup brandy	¾ cup liquid coffee
15 ounces unsweetened chocolate	3¼ cups heavy cream

CRUST:

8 ounces semisweet chocolate	½ teaspoon almond extract
6 tablespoons unsalted butter	2 cups toasted chopped almonds

TO MAKE FILLING: Beat yolks in top of double boiler with 1½ cups sugar, vanilla and brandy over simmering water until mixture is thick. Remove from water and set aside.

Melt chocolates over hot water or over very low direct heat carefully. Remove and beat in butter a little at a time. Gradually beat chocolate into yolks until mixture is smooth. Beat in coffee.

Beat whites until soft peaks form. Gradually beat in 3 tablespoons sugar until stiff peaks form. Beat 1 cup whites into chocolate mixture. Then fold in remaining whites, blending well. Whip 2¼ cups cream until stiff and fold into chocolate mixture. Pour into prepared crusts and freeze or refrigerate.

TO MAKE CRUST: In top of double boiler over hot water or carefully over direct heat melt chocolate and butter. Stir in almond extract and almonds. Chill about 30 minutes, until mixture is thick enough to spread on bottom of two buttered 8-inch springform pans. Chill until hardened and then fill.

NOTE TO COOK: Carry to party in springform molds. Unmold at party and place on serving trays. Carry remaining 1 cup heavy cream to party and whip before decorating cakes.

Mushroom caviar
Zucchini pancakes

Cold Chinese noodle salad

Shaking beef cubes
Steamed asparagus
Red pepper puree

"Kugelhopf"
Almond crescents

Cooking facilities needed: oven and top of the stove
Silverware needed: forks, knives, spoons

This dinner is really designed for a smallish group that can sit down at a table or tables to eat it. It also requires last-minute cooking of the food and last-minute preparation of the salad. The hors d'oeuvres are served with cocktails, the noodles as a first course, the salad after the beef and asparagus.

It is the perfect kind of cooperative dinner for people who like to cook together or for just two people to give together.

If six people, however, are going to cook it, the person who does the mushroom caviar should probably also have responsibility for the asparagus.

Mushroom caviar (R2)   (12 SERVINGS AS HORS D'OEUVRE)

3 medium onions, minced

5 tablespoons good-quality olive oil

1½ pounds fresh mushrooms

3¼ to 4 teaspoons ground coriander seeds

Salt and freshly ground black pepper to taste

Fresh parsley, chopped for garnish

Thinly sliced black bread

Cook onions in hot oil until soft. Chop mushrooms finely; add to pan with coriander, salt and pepper and cook until mushrooms let off their juice; turn up heat and cook so most of liquid evaporates. Refrigerate until chilled. Adjust seasoning if necessary. Decorate with chopped parsley and serve with thinly sliced black bread.

NOTE TO COOK: Prepare recipe and carry to party in serving bowl, already decorated with parsley. Carry bread separately and arrange on plate at party.

Zucchini pancakes (RI)   (2 TO 2½ DOZEN)

1 pound 2 ounces zucchini
2 ounces cream cheese, softened
¼ cup freshly grated Parmesan cheese
2 tablespoons flour
1 tablespoon chopped fresh chives (optional)

Freshly ground black pepper to taste
2 eggs
Oil for sautéing
Sour cream or Crème Fraîche (see page 172) for topping— approximately 1 to 1½ cups

Scrub zucchini and trim off ends. Shred coarsely in food processor or by hand. Let stand for 30 minutes in strainer. Place small amounts of drained zucchini in cloth kitchen towel and twist to squeeze out excess moisture.

Meanwhile beat together cream cheese, Parmesan cheese, flour, optional chives, pepper and eggs, mixing well. Beat in zucchini.

Heat a large skillet and film with oil. Drop batter by heaping teaspoons onto hot skillet and fry until golden brown; turn and brown on second side. Repeat until all pancakes are cooked. Drain each batch on paper towels. If being served immediately, keep warm in oven until all are prepared. Or prepare ahead and refrigerate.

To serve, reheat pancakes on cookie sheet at 400 degrees for 5 to 10 minutes or until they are very hot.

Serve with sour cream or crème fraîche as topping or dip.

NOTE TO COOK: Prepare pancakes ahead and bring to party on cookie sheet, wrapped in foil. Remove foil and reheat at party. Carry sour cream or crème fraîche in small serving bowl or covered container. At party arrange zucchini on serving tray with bowl of sour cream or crème fraîche in the center. Serve with toothpicks.

These are also delicious for breakfast or brunch made about twice the size.

Crème fraîche (R7)

1 pint heavy cream*   2 tablespoons buttermilk

Pour cream into a jar. Stir in buttermilk. Cover loosely. Leave in warm place, such as on top of the stove, until cream thickens like yogurt. This can take as little as twenty-four hours or as long as four days.

Store in refrigerator for up to two or three weeks.

* Do not use ultrapasteurized cream. It will not work.

Cold Chinese noodle salad (R1)

(12 FIRST-COURSE SERVINGS)

24 ounces Chinese noodles, preferably fresh †

1½ tablespoons Oriental sesame oil †

9 tablespoons brewed tea or water

6 tablespoons dark soy sauce

6 tablespoons sesame seed paste †

3 tablespoons peanut oil

3 tablespoons dry sherry

2 tablespoons red wine vinegar

1 tablespoon sugar

6 garlic cloves, mashed to a paste

1½-inch piece fresh ginger, mashed

4½ teaspoons chili oil †

Freshly ground black pepper to taste

Chopped scallion

Cook the noodles in boiling water for 2 to 4 minutes. Test frequently so they don't overcook. Drain well and toss with sesame oil. Refrigerate, covered, at least 2 hours, overnight if desired.

Combine all remaining ingredients except scallion and mix well. Since the sesame paste is often very difficult to mix well, you can put it in a food processor with steel knife and some of the liquid. Add the garlic and ginger, and while the sesame paste is being blended, the garlic and ginger will be finely minced.

If the sauce is not being used immediately, it can be refrigerated, but before serving over noodles, bring to room temperature. Stir noodles with sauce and serve topped with scallion.

NOTE TO COOK: Carry noodles mixed with sauce to party in serving bowl tightly covered with plastic or in container with tight-fitting lid. Carry chopped scallion separately. Just before serving, toss noodles and sprinkle with scallion.

† All ingredients available at Oriental market. If fresh Chinese noodles are not available, use American dried spaghettini or linguine and cook according to package directions.

The Oriental sesame paste is preferable to tahini because it has a toasted flavor, but tahini can be substituted.

This recipe, adapted from one created by Germaine Swanson, owner of Ge. maine's Restaurant in Washington, D.C., derives its name from the shaking the pan is given when the meat is cooked.

MARINADE:

1 tablespoon chopped garlic

3 tablespoons finely chopped shallots

3 tablespoons Maggi sauce

3 tablespoons imported light Chinese or Japanese soy sauce

White pepper to taste

4½ pounds filet mignon or strip steaks, thoroughly trimmed of fat and cut into ¾-inch cubes

3 medium onions, thinly sliced and separated into rings

DRESSING:

3 small red onions, finely sliced

1 teaspoon finely chopped garlic

Few dashes white pepper

3 tablespoons distilled white vinegar

6 tablespoons vegetable oil

3 large heads Boston lettuce

TO FINISH

½ cup vegetable oil

6 tablespoons butter

Combine ingredients for marinade and add cubes of meat, stirring to coat meat well with marinade. Allow to marinate at room temperature at least 20 minutes, overnight, if desired.

Combine dressing ingredients.

Wash and dry lettuce, breaking up into individual leaves. Arrange lettuce on large serving platter and before cooking the meat, mix dressing and pour over lettuce.

Place large skillet(s) over high heat and add oil. When oil begins to smoke, add drained meat cubes and sliced onions. Stir-fry very quickly and shake the pan until the meat is brown on the outside but rare inside. Turn off heat; add butter; swirl and spoon immediately over lettuce-lined platter.

NOTE TO COOK: Carry the marinade and meat to party in one tightly covered container. Carry sliced onions in plastic bag. Carry dressing in another container. Carry vegetable oil and butter in original containers and carry lettuce, washed and dried, in plastic bag.

Arrange lettuce on serving platter and pour over dressing. When it is time to serve, cook meat and onions according to directions.

173

Steamed asparagus

6 pounds asparagus

Wash and trim asparagus by breaking off tough bottom stems. Steam over boiling water for about 10 minutes, until asparagus are tender but still crisp.

NOTE TO COOK: Cleaned asparagus and possibly steamer, if hostess doesn't have one, should be carried to party. Put the water on in the steamer to boil when beef is ready to be cooked.

Red pepper puree (R1)

12 large red bell peppers
4 to 6 tablespoons olive oil
1 to 1½ teaspoons dried thyme

Freshly ground black pepper to taste
Few dashes cayenne

To remove skin from peppers either broil or hold on fork over gas flame. For this many peppers it is easier to broil them.

Line broiling pans with aluminum foil and place peppers on foil three or four inches from source of heat. Turn them on all sides, on top and bottom as the skin blisters and blackens. When it is blistered and blackened all over, remove the peppers and place in plastic bag. Keep bag closed and allow the peppers to steam in the bag for 10 or 15 minutes. (The peppers will be done at different times: just take each from the broiler as it is ready and place in the bag.)

Check the bag after 10 minutes to see if the skin will come off easily. Using your fingers and a small knife remove the skin then seed peppers. Cut each pepper into five or six pieces.

Heat oil in one or more skillets and when it is hot add thyme and peppers. Sauté about two minutes; season with black pepper and cayenne.

Puree peppers in food processor with steel blade or in blender. Refrigerate. To serve, reheat slowly.

NOTE TO COOK: Carry to party in tightly covered container and reheat about five minutes before serving time. Stir to prevent sticking.

This is not a traditional kugelhopf; it is a meringue baked in a kugelhopf mold, a specialty from François Haeringer at L'Auberge Chez François in Great Falls, Virginia, just outside Washington, D.C. Directions must be followed to the letter and a kugelhopf mold or Bundt pan is essential or the dessert will not work. I know. I tried it three times without a mold.

½ cup golden raisins

2 tablespoons kirsch

½ teaspoon unflavored gelatin

2 tablespoons water

12 egg whites

2 tablespoons grated orange rind (2 oranges)

2 teaspoons grated lemon rind

1 teaspoon vanilla extract

1¼ cups sugar

Caramel Glaze (see page 176)

Strawberry halves for garnish (optional)

Combine raisins and kirsch and allow to macerate at room temperature at least an hour, longer if desired.

Soften gelatin in water in small saucepan; stir to mix; dissolve over very low heat. In large mixing bowl combine egg whites, orange and lemon rinds, gelatin, vanilla and ½ teaspoon of the kirsch from the raisins. Beat with electric mixer at high speed, just until foamy white. Add sugar a few tablespoons at a time and continue beating until meringue mixture forms stiff glossy peaks. Drain off remaining kirsch and fold raisins into meringue.

Spoon mixture into a buttered and sugared 12-cup kugelhopf mold or 10-inch Bundt pan. Cut through the mixture with a spatula to break up any large air bubbles; smooth top. Place pan in a larger, deeper pan; put both pans on bottom shelf of oven that has been heated to 300 degrees. Pull shelf out and pour boiling water into outer pan to the depth of 3 or 4 inches up the side of the tube pan.

Bake for 30 minutes. Then tent a piece of foil over top of the pan if dessert is browning too fast. Bake 15 to 25 minutes longer, or until cake tester inserted in center comes out without any of the meringue clinging to it. Remove pan from water to wire rack. Run knife around the outer edge and the inside tube to loosen. This keeps dessert from tearing as it cools and shrinks. Cool completely in pan.

When dessert is cooled, run knife around edges again and carefully remove from pan directly onto serving plate. The dessert can be made to this point the morning of the day it will be served and refrigerated. The glaze may be made a few hours before serving.

When you are ready to make the glaze, remove kugelhopf from refrigerator.

Caramel glaze

½ cup sugar   ½ cup water

Combine sugar and water in small saucepan. Cook, stirring occasionally, until sugar melts and caramelizes to a golden brown. Watch very carefully: The difference between golden brown and burnt is only a matter of seconds. Immediately drizzle over the kugelhopf. Do not wait or the caramel will get too dark and begin to harden.

Refrigerate, uncovered. Decorate with strawberry halves, if desired.

NOTE TO COOK: This dessert is not easy to transport but it can be done: I have. It cannot be covered unless you have the kind of cake plate with cover that will not touch the meringue. Otherwise the meringue pulls away. You will have to hold it in your lap on your way to the party. But it's worth it. Carry strawberry halves separately. Refrigerate at party. Decorate it with the halved strawberries before serving.

PAGE 187

Almond crescents (F/R2)   (ABOUT 60)

1¼ cups toasted ground almonds   1 teaspoon vanilla extract
 1 cup unsalted butter, softened   1 teaspoon almond extract
 ½ cup sugar   2 cups unbleached flour

Toast almonds and grind. Cream butter. Gradually add sugar and beat until light and fluffy. Add vanilla and almond extracts.

Stir in the flour and nuts, mixing to blend well. Form dough into ball and wrap in waxed papper. Chill for 1 hour.

Using 1 teaspoon of dough, shape into crescents 2 to 3 inches long. Place on ungreased baking sheets about an inch apart. Bake at 350 degrees for 15 minutes, or until crescents are light golden in color.

Freeze if desired or store in tightly covered container at room temperature. To serve, defrost if frozen.

NOTE TO COOK: Carry to party in container in which the cookies were stored. Arrange on serving tray at party.

Smoked mozzarella and sun-dried tomatoes

Lecso with sausages
Cumin beef balls
Lentils and goat cheese salad
Buttermilk potato salad

Zabaglione semifreddo with strawberries

Cooking facilities needed: top of stove
Silverware needed: forks, spoons

This is a perfect dinner for a small kitchen; only the lecso has to be re-heated. Nothing else requires cooking. It's also a good menu for a hot night since the kitchen won't get heated up.

Smoked mozzarella and sun-dried tomatoes (R3) (12 SERVINGS)

1 cup olive oil
½ cup dry white wine
24 peppercorns
1 teaspoon dried basil

1 teaspoon dried oregano leaves
½ pound sun-dried tomatoes
1 pound smoked mozzarella cheese, cut in ½-inch cubes

Bring the oil, wine, peppercorns, basil and oregano to boil in a non-aluminum pot. Stir in tomatoes and simmer for 10 minutes, until tomatoes soften. Remove from heat; cover and let mixture sit for an hour. Pour off all but ½ cup of the liquid and combine with tomatoes and mozzarella; stir gently and serve at room temperature. This mixture is better if made a few days in advance. Serve with toothpicks.

NOTE TO COOK: Carry to party in tightly covered plastic container. Arrange on serving dish with toothpicks at party.

Sun-dried tomatoes and smoked mozzarella are found in Italian grocery stores and gourmet food shops. Smoked mozzarella bears no relationship to that bouncy stuff they sell as mozzarella in the supermarket.

Lecso with sausages (RI)

Called Serbian goulash, stewed peppers and tomatoes, this is a wonderful Hungarian dish. It is served as an appetizer or side dish and with the addition of sausages becomes a main dish.

Hungarian sausage is difficult to find so substitute kielbasa, the Polish sausage.

10 large green peppers, about 5 pounds

8 large ripe tomatoes, about 5 pounds

8 tablespoons drippings from nitrite-free bacon

4 large onions, chopped

4 cloves garlic, minced

¼ cup Hungarian sweet paprika

1 tablespoon caraway seeds

Salt to taste

2 pounds spicy sausage (like kielbasa), cut in ⅛-inch-thick slices

Core and seed peppers and cut into rings. Dip tomatoes in boiling water or hold over flame to loosen skin; peel and cut in chunks.

Sauté onions and garlic in bacon drippings until soft, about 10 minutes. Add paprika and stir well. Stir in peppers, tomatoes and salt, if desired. Simmer, covered, about 30 minutes, until peppers are very tender.

Meanwhile, brown the sausages and add to lecso.

NOTE TO COOK: Prepare lecso at home and carry to party in cooking pot. Reheat and spoon into serving dish.

Cumin beef balls (RI)

These are both Greek and Armenian. In Greece they are called soutzoukakia. I have adapted them.

1 cup fresh whole-wheat bread crumbs

6 tablespoons finely chopped parsley

2 pounds ground beef

2 medium onions

1 tablespoon ground cumin

Salt and freshly ground black pepper to taste

Vegetable oil for sautéing

Using steel blade of food processor, process bread crumbs finely, chop parsley, chop onion, finely grind beef.

Mix beef, onions, bread crumbs, parsley, cumin, salt and pepper. Shape balls approximately 1 inch in diameter. Heat a little oil in a heavy skillet, just enough to film the bottom of the skillet. Brown beef balls on all sides in hot oil. Drain on paper toweling. Serve at room temperature.

NOTE TO COOK: These beef balls can be prepared a day ahead and cooked an hour or two before going to the party. Do not refrigerate. Carry to party either in serving bowl or on jelly-roll pan, tightly covered.

Lentils and goat cheese salad (R2)   (12 SERVINGS)

This is adapted from a dish served at Green's, a natural-food restaurant overlooking the bay in San Francisco.

2 cups (16 ounces) lentils

1 cup finely diced carrots

1 cup finely diced red onions

Bouquet garni of ½ teaspoon dried thyme leaves, 1 bay leaf, 8 peppercorns and 4 whole cloves tied in cheesecloth

4 large cloves garlic, chopped

5 cups water

Salt and freshly ground black pepper to taste

6 tablespoons olive oil

4 tablespoons plus 2 teaspoons red wine vinegar

Thinly sliced red onion for garnish, about 1 onion

Small chunks goat cheese such as Montrachet or boucheron for garnish, about 6 ounces

Combine lentils, carrots, diced red onion, bouquet garni, garlic and water in large pot and simmer until lentils are tender but not mushy. They should hold their shape. Drain off liquid; remove bouquet garni and season lentils with salt and pepper, olive oil and vinegar. Refrigerate, if desired. To serve, toss with slices of red onion and chunks of goat cheese.

NOTE TO COOK: Carry to party in salad bowl, or carry in plastic container.

Buttermilk potato salad (RI)

1 cup olive oil
6 large cloves garlic, minced
¾ cup buttermilk or yogurt
Juice of 1 lemon
1 teaspoon grated lemon peel
2 tablespoons sesame seeds
2 tablespoons caraway seeds

1 cup chopped parsley
1 teaspoon dry mustard
Salt and freshly ground black pepper to taste
6 pounds, cooked, peeled and coarsely diced potatoes

Combine all ingredients but potatoes and mix thoroughly. Stir in potatoes carefully and chill. The longer the potatoes are mixed with the salad, the more they absorb the flavors of the dressing. This is a good dish to make a day ahead.

The dressing is also good with other cold vegetables, like carrots or broccoli.

NOTE TO COOK: Carry to party in tightly covered plastic container or in serving bowl, well wrapped.

Zabaglione semifreddo (F)
(SOFT FROZEN ZABAGLIONE)
(12 SERVINGS)

12 egg yolks
1 cup granulated sugar
Grated peel of 1 lemon
1 tablespoon vanilla extract

1 cup Marsala wine
1 pint heavy cream, whipped
5 dozen strawberries for garnish

Mix yolks with sugar. Beat in lemon peel, vanilla and wine. Cook over very low heat or over hot water in top of double boiler, beating constantly with wire whisk until mixture thickens to custardlike consistency.

Beat cream until stiff. Fold whipped cream into yolk mixture and pour into large serving bowl. Wrap well and place in the freezer overnight.

To serve, remove from freezer and top with strawberries.

NOTE TO COOK: Carry zabaglione in serving dish, well wrapped, to party. Store in freezer. Carry strawberries separately and serve in separate dish alongside the zabaglione.

Creamy stuffed mushrooms
Onion sandwiches

Corn and beef pie
Chicken and apricot salad
Carrots, ginger and cumin
Italian rice and vegetable salad

Grapefruit sorbet
Willard Scott's brown sugar pound cake

Cooking facilities needed: top of stove, oven   *Silverware needed: forks, spoons*

A good menu for a small kitchen. Very little last-minute work.

Creamy stuffed mushrooms (R1)   (ABOUT 40)

1 pound small mushrooms (bite-size or a little larger)

2 teaspoons Worcestershire sauce

¼ teaspoon paprika

1 teaspoon lemon juice

1 tablespoon minced fresh parsley

3 or 4 rolled anchovy fillets, drained and mashed or cut fine

2 ounces cream cheese, softened

¼ cup sour cream

Additional chopped fresh parsley for garnish

Remove stems from mushroom caps, wash, trim and chop stems very fine. Mix stems together with Worcestershire, paprika, lemon juice, parsley and anchovies. Blend cream cheese and sour cream together and add to first mixture; mix well.

Stuff mushroom caps. Refrigerate.

NOTE TO COOK: Carry stuffed mushrooms to party in storage container or on serving dish, wrapped with a tent of aluminum foil. Decorate each with a touch of parsley.

181

Onion sandwiches (RI)

1 loaf thin-sliced white bread

5 tablespoons unsalted butter, at room temperature

1 cup homemade mayonnaise

2 cups very thinly sliced sweet onion, such as Bermuda or Vidalia

Salt and pepper to taste

Butter half the bread slices on one side and spread mayonnaise thinly on one side of remaining slices. Place one layer of onion slices on the bread slices spread with mayonnaise; top onions with additional mayonnaise; season with salt and pepper. Top with buttered bread.

Cut off crusts and cut each sandwich in half lengthwise. Cover tightly and chill well.

NOTE TO COOK: Carry to party either in storage container or arranged on serving tray.

Corn and beef pie (RI)

5 tablespoons vegetable oil

3 medium onions, finely chopped

3 canned tomatoes, chopped, or 2 large fresh tomatoes, finely chopped

5 cloves garlic, pressed or minced

1¼ cups diced pimiento-stuffed olives

1¼ cups raisins

1¼ teaspoons crushed red pepper

3 teaspoons ground cumin

2½ teaspoons paprika

2 pounds lean ground beef

1¼ cups bulgur

Freshly ground pepper and salt to taste

3 pounds frozen corn kernels

1½ cups thinly sliced scallions

5 eggs

2½ tablespoons flour

¾ cup low-fat or regular milk

Heat 2½ tablespoons oil in large skillet. Sauté onion, tomatoes and garlic until vegetables are softened and liquid from tomatoes has evaporated. Stir in olives, raisins and spices. Mix in beef, bulgur, salt and pepper to taste. Spread mixture into bottom and sides of 2 10x15-inch ovenproof casseroles.

Meanwhile, heat the remaining oil in a skillet and sauté corn and scallions until scallions soften, just a minute or two. Drain off corn liquid. Spoon mixture into meat pie crusts.

At this point the crusts may be refrigerated until serving time. To serve, allow to return to room temperature for 20 minutes. Beat together eggs and flour until smooth. Beat in milk. Pour over corn and bake at 350 degrees 20 to 30 minutes, until eggs are set.

Important: Cool for 10 minutes before serving for best flavor.

NOTE TO COOK: If you live very close to the party, you can bake the pies, cover with aluminum foil and transport to party already baked. They will keep warm in the foil for about 45 minutes. Or carry crusts to party well wrapped. Mix the eggs, flour and milk and carry to party in storage container. At party pour milk mixture into crusts and bake.

Chicken and apricot salad (RI)   (16 SERVINGS)

¾ cup homemade mayonnaise
2 cups plain yogurt
2 tablespoons lemon juice
½ teaspoon dry mustard
2 cups diced dried apricots
6 cups diced cooked white-meat chicken

1 cup chopped walnuts, toasted
½ cup finely chopped scallions
Dried apricots for garnish, soft green lettuce or additional scallions for garnish

Blend mayonnaise, yogurt, lemon juice and mustard in a bowl. Add apricots, chicken, walnuts and scallions and mix well. Chill and serve on lettuce leaves.

Sprinkle with additional scallions or diced apricots for color.

NOTE TO COOK: Carry to party in storage container, carrying garnishes in plastic bags. Arrange at party. Or carry salad to party on lettuce leaves in serving bowl or platter wrapped with plastic, garnishing with scallions or apricots at party.

Carrots, ginger and cumin (RI) (16 SERVINGS)

3 pounds carrots

2 tablespoons ground cumin seed

1 cup unsalted butter

3 tablespoons chopped fresh ginger

6 cloves garlic, chopped

6 tablespoons lemon juice

1½ cups low-fat or regular milk

Salt and freshly ground black pepper to taste

Scrape the carrots and cut into medium slices or slice in food processor. Cook carrots in boiling salted water until just tender, about 5 minutes, depending on thickness of carrots. Drain and rinse under cold water to stop cooking.

Meanwhile, sauté the cumin in 1 tablespoon of the butter for 30 seconds. Add the ginger and garlic and sauté 1 minute longer. Combine the cooked, drained carrots with the cumin-garlic mixture, the lemon juice, remaining butter and milk, and process in food processor with steel blade, in batches, until smooth. Season with salt and freshly ground pepper. To serve, heat through.

NOTE TO COOK: Carry to party in storage container. Reheat at party and place in serving dish.

Italian rice and vegetable salad (RI) (16 SERVINGS)

DRESSING:

3 large cloves garlic, minced

6 anchovies, mashed, or 6 strips anchovy paste, each about ½ inch long

1½ teaspoons dried oregano

1½ teaspoons dried basil

1½ teaspoons dry mustard

Juice of 3 lemons

Freshly ground black pepper to taste

6 tablespoons red wine vinegar

1 cup good-quality olive oil

SALAD:

3 tablespoons olive oil

3 cups arborio or long-grain rice

6 cups boiling water

1½ cups roasted red peppers, julienned

36 Italian or French black olives, pitted and halved

1 cup pine nuts, toasted

1 cup fresh fennel, coarsely chopped

3 10-ounce packages frozen peas (or fresh peas if available)

184

DRESSING: Mash garlic with anchovies or anchovy paste and mix with oregano, basil, mustard, lemon juice and pepper. Whisk in vinegar and then whisk in olive oil.

SALAD: Heat oil in skillet and add rice. Sauté, stirring, until rice begins to brown. Turn heat to low and add boiling water. Stir, cover and simmer arborio rice for 5 minutes, long-grain rice for 10 minutes. Remove rice and allow to steam for 4 minutes with cover on. In strainer drain rice of any remaining liquid and spread on cookie sheet to dry. Then place in large bowl and add all but about 6 tablespoons of the dressing. Mix carefully. Add red peppers and olives. Cover and refrigerate if desired.

An hour before serving, remove rice from refrigerator. Defrost frozen peas and cook about a minute or two in their own moisture; drain. Add with pine nuts and fennel to rice. Add remaining dressing and toss carefully. Adjust seasoning and serve, in glass bowl if available.

This salad is best at room temperature.

NOTE TO COOK: Carry mixed salad to party in storage container or serving bowl, wrapped with plastic wrap.

Grapefruit sorbet (F) (16 SERVINGS)

2 cups sugar	12 cups fresh pink grapefruit
2 cups water	juice

Combine sugar and water; boil for 5 minutes; cool. Squeeze grapefruits and combine the juice with approximately 2 cups sugar syrup, depending on sweetness desired. Freeze in sorbet maker, ice cream maker or in ice cube trays of refrigerator freezer. If the last method is used, thaw slightly after freezing and beat in mixer or food processor; repeat this procedure twice and freeze until serving time. Just before serving, beat again.

Willard Scott's brown sugar pound cake

(Cake F/R1; Cake and frosting R1)   (16 SERVINGS)

When Willard Scott of the "Today" show was the weatherman at WRC-TV, NBC's television station in Washington, D.C., one charitable organization that he plugged each year sent him this unbelievably rich cake, which all of us at the station devoured, and somehow or other the recipe became *his*.

½ pound unsalted butter, room temperature
½ cup shortening
5 eggs, room temperature
1 pound plus 1 cup light brown sugar

3½ cups unbleached flour
½ teaspoon baking powder
1 cup milk

Cream together butter and shortening. Add eggs, one at a time, creaming after each addition. Add sugar and beat well.

Sift together flour and baking powder. Add flour mixture alternately with milk to sugar mixture. Bake in greased and floured 10-inch tube pan at 325 degrees for 1 hour and 10 minutes to 1 hour and 30 minutes. Cool in pan on wire rack. Remove cooled cake. Freeze or refrigerate, if desired. To frost, return to room temperature if frozen.

Spread Pecan Frosting on top of cooled cake.

PECAN FROSTING:

1 cup chopped pecans
¼ pound unsalted butter

1 pound box confectioners' sugar
Milk to thin

Toast pecans in butter until they brown. Let cool a little, then mix with confectioners' sugar. Add enough milk to thin to spreading consistency. Spread on top of cooled cake. Some of the frosting should drip down the sides and center, but should be spread only on the top. Refrigerate, if desired.

NOTE TO COOK: Carry cake to party either in cake tray that has its own lid or very carefully tented with aluminum foil so that foil does not touch the frosting.

Guacamole
Sesame-coated Muenster gin ball

Baked chicken with coriander
Eggplant "dressing" with shrimp and rice
Bulgur with red onion
Green beans and goat cheese salad

Almond tartes

Cooking facilities needed: oven and top of stove   *Silverware needed: forks, knives*

Ask one person to make the rice, another to make the Eggplant "dressing."

Guacamole

(3 CUPS)

2 medium very ripe avocados
2 medium ripe tomatoes
1 small onion, finely minced
1 or 2 small hot chiles, minced
1 teaspoon each lemon and lime juice
Salt and freshly ground black pepper to taste

¾ teaspoon ground coriander seed
Fresh coriander (cilantro or Chinese parsley) for garnish (optional)
Fried tortilla chips

Mash avocado with fork slightly. Add tomatoes, onion and chiles and chop finely. Add remaining ingredients and adjust seasonings to taste.

Serve with fried tortilla chips (tostaditas).

NOTE TO COOK: This must be made, if not at the last minute, at least within a few hours of serving.

Prepare all ingredients except the avocado and mix. Carry to party in storage container along with avocados and chips. At party, mash avocados and mix with remaining ingredients. Garnish with optional coriander leaves and serve with tortilla chips. Or, if you live close to the party, you can prepare the dish at home, sprinkle top with additional lemon or lime juice and carry to party in serving bowl tightly wrapped with plastic. Carry optional coriander leaves separately. At party, stir guacamole, decorate with leaves and serve.

Sesame-coated Muenster gin ball (R2) (16 SERVINGS)

¾ pound Muenster cheese, cut into chunks

6 tablespoons unsalted butter, softened

1½ tablespoons coarse-grain mustard

3 tablespoons gin

1½ ounces toasted sesame seeds

Crackers and/or crudités such as celery, zucchini

In a food processor with steel blade combine cheese, butter, mustard and gin and blend until smooth. Chill until mixture is firm enough to shape into a ball. Roll in toasted sesame seeds.

Serve with crackers and/or raw vegetables.

NOTE TO COOK: Prepare cheese ball and carry to party in serving dish with a tent of aluminum foil or in storage container. Carry crackers in original boxes and, if serving crudités, prepare them ahead and carry them in plastic bags. Arrange at party.

Baked chicken with coriander (F/RI) (16 SERVINGS)

3 tablespoons ground coriander

Freshly ground black pepper and salt to taste

16 chicken breast halves

Flour

¾ cup vegetable oil

4 large onions, finely chopped

4 6-ounce cans tomato paste

2 cups dry sherry

½ cup minced fresh basil or 8 teaspoons dried basil

Fresh coriander (cilantro or Chinese parsley) or parsley for garnish

Combine coriander and pepper and rub into chicken pieces. Dredge chicken in flour that has been seasoned with salt to taste. Heat oil in large skillet(s) and sauté chicken pieces until they are golden brown on both sides. Place chicken pieces in one or more shallow casseroles so that they are in a single layer.

Sauté onion in oil remaining in skillet until soft. Spoon onion over chicken. Stir sherry into tomato paste and mix with basil. Pour over chicken pieces.

Freeze or refrigerate if desired. To serve, return to room temperature and bake, covered, at 350 degrees 30 to 45 minutes, until chicken is tender.

NOTE TO COOK: Just before leaving, bake chicken at home for 15 to 20 minutes and carry to party in baking dish. Finish the baking, 15 to 25 minutes at the party or bake completely at party. Serve decorated with fresh coriander or parsley.

Eggplant "dressing" with shrimp and rice (R1)   (16 SERVINGS)

This is a variation of a Cajun recipe served at Patout's Restaurant in Lafayette, Louisiana. It is usually served over fried eggplant. To simplify, it is being served over rice here. This isn't "dressing" such as one expects to find in a turkey.

2 pounds raw shrimp	½ teaspoon dried thyme leaves
¾ pound butter	½ teaspoon dried basil
6 medium-large onions, finely chopped	½ teaspoon dried oregano
4 green peppers, finely chopped	1 pound crabmeat
2 stalks celery, finely chopped	½ cup each chopped scallions and parsley
4 large eggplants	2½ cups brown or white rice, cooked
1½ teaspoons cayenne	
1½ teaspoons white pepper	
1½ teaspoons black pepper	
Salt to taste	

Peel shrimp and set aside. Cover shells with 4 cups water; boil until reduced to 2 cups. Strain; set stock aside.

Heat butter in large skillet; cook onions, peppers and celery slowly in hot butter for 15 minutes, until mixture is soft.

Peel and cut eggplants into ¾-inch cubes; place in saucepan with water to cover halfway up eggplants. Cook until cubes are tender, about 7 minutes. Drain and remove as much water as possible. Puree. Add eggplant puree, shrimp stock and seasonings to sautéed vegetables; cook over medium-low heat about 20 minutes.

At this point the dish may be refrigerated and finished just before serving.

If refrigerated, reheat eggplant mixture. Add shrimp; cook 7 to 10 minutes over moderately high heat, until shrimp is pink. Add crabmeat; heat through. Stir in scallions and parsley. Serve over rice.

NOTE TO COOK: Prepare dressing at home up to the point where shrimp is added. Carry dressing to party in cooking pot. Carry shrimp, crabmeat and chopped scallions and parsley separately. Finish cooking at party. Cook rice at home and reheat either over hot water or covered in oven while chicken is baking at party.

Bulgur with red onion (R1)

2½ cups bulgur

¾ cup vegetable oil

4 teaspoons sesame oil

7½ tablespoons lemon juice

½ cup plus 2 tablespoons finely chopped fresh mint

1½ cups minced fresh parsley

2 medium red onions, coarsely chopped

1 teaspoon ground coriander

1 teaspoon ground cumin

Freshly ground black pepper to taste

Fresh mint leaves for garnish

Soak bulgur in water to cover for 15 minutes. Drain in colander and then squeeze bulgur to drain out as much moisture as possible. Combine remaining ingredients and whisk. Pour over bulgur and mix to coat. Allow to stand at room temperature at least 1 hour before serving. Or refrigerate but return to room temperature before serving.

NOTE TO COOK: Carry to party in serving bowl or storage container. Carry mint leaves separately and decorate bulgur at party.

Green beans and goat cheese salad (R1)

4½ pounds fresh green beans, ends trimmed

1 cup plus 2 tablespoons olive oil

¾ cup white wine vinegar

3 cloves garlic, crushed

Freshly ground black pepper to taste

2 cups chopped toasted pecans

1½ cups coarsely grated hard goat cheese or imported Parmesan

Steam green beans about 7 to 9 minutes, until crisp-tender. Drain.

While beans are cooking, combine oil and vinegar and beat. Add garlic and pepper. Mix drained, warm beans with dressing and allow to sit about 10 minutes, longer if desired. If beans will not be served within an hour or two, refrigerate, but return to room temperature before serving.

Just before serving, sprinkle beans with toasted pecans and grated cheese.

NOTE TO COOK: Carry marinated beans to party either in serving dish covered tightly with plastic wrap or in storage container. Carry grated cheese and toasted pecans in separate containers. Just before serving, finish dressing salad with cheese and pecans.

This is a rich dessert, so very small slices are in order. If, however, you think your guests want large slices, make two tartes. This is an adaptation of one given to me by Chez Panisse.

CRUSTS:

2 tablespoons sugar

2 cups flour

1 cup unsalted butter

2 tablespoons water

Few drops almond extract

1 teaspoon vanilla extract

Combine sugar and flour and cut in butter until mixture is fine-grained. Add water, almond and vanilla extracts and toss to incorporate and make into 2 balls. Press each evenly into 2 9-inch tart pans that have been lined with waxed paper. Chill 1 hour.

Bake at 400 degrees for 10 minutes. Press down any crust that puffs up.

FILLING:

2 cups sliced unblanched almonds

1½ cups sugar

1½ cups heavy cream

Salt to taste

Few drops almond extract

2 teaspoons Grand Marnier

Whipped cream for topping (optional)

Combine all ingredients except whipped cream and allow to stand in warm place for 20 minutes to dissolve sugar. Pour into prepared shells and bake at 400 degrees for 30 to 40 minutes, until tops brown and caramelize. Keep turning in oven to brown evenly.

Refrigerate, if desired, but serve at room temperature. If desired, top with puffs of whipped cream.

NOTE TO COOK: Carry to party in tart pans, covered with aluminum foil. If using whipped cream, carry cream separately and whip at party. Remove from tart pans at party and place on serving trays. Top with whipped cream.

Cheese straws
Seafood and basil phyllo

Marinated lamb Hunan style
Rice with dried fruits and nuts
Salad of red pepper and celery root
Bundles of spinach

Ventana chocolate torte

Last-minute finishing in oven and on top of stove   *Silverware needed: forks*

This menu calls for each of seven people to make a single dish or for one person to take on two. The easiest for one person, in terms of time, would be the rice and salad.

Cheese straws (F/R3)   (APPROXIMATELY 9 DOZEN)

1 pound extra-sharp cheddar cheese	1½ sticks unsalted butter
1¾ cups unbleached flour	Few dashes cayenne

Grate cheese on grater or in food processor. If using food processor, add remaining ingredients and combine using steel blade. (In a smaller processor you will have to do this in two batches.)

Chill dough overnight or for 8 hours. Divide into 3 or 4 portions. Soften just enough to roll out ⅛ to ¼ inch thick between two sheets of waxed paper. Using a knife or a tool with a serrated edge, cut dough into strips 3 inches long and less than an inch wide. Rechill scraps before rerolling. Place on ungreased cookie sheets and bake at 400 degrees about 10 minutes, until the dough takes on a barely tan color. Watch carefully.

Freeze or store in airtight container.

NOTE TO COOK: Bring to party in container and arrange on serving dish at party.

You will not need 9 dozen, but these keep very well and are always nice to have for unexpected drop-ins or to take somewhere.

¼ pound shrimp, cooked, shelled and chopped

6 tablespoons freshly grated Parmesan cheese

9 fresh basil leaves or 1½ tablespoons dried, crumbled basil

6 ounces cream cheese

2 tablespoons dry sherry
Few shakes nutmeg

¼ pound crabmeat

½ pound phyllo, preferably fresh, not frozen

¼ to ½ pound unsalted butter, approximately

Chop shrimp in food processor. Place cheese in processor with steel blade. Process until cheese is grated. Add fresh basil and process to mince basil. Add cream cheese, sherry and nutmeg and process. Stir into crab and shrimp.

Cut phyllo lengthwise into 4 strips. Place on damp cloth and cover with waxed paper and another damp cloth to prevent sheets from drying out. Working with one or two strips at a time, brush with melted butter. Fold over about a ¼ inch from the bottom edge. Add a spoonful of the filling just above fold and fold again to form a triangle. The folding is done as if you were folding an American flag.

Place seam side down on baking sheets. When all the triangles have been made, brush tops with melted butter. Bake at 400 degrees for 20 to 30 minutes, until tops are browned.

Freeze or refrigerate if desired. To serve, defrost if frozen and reheat at 350 degrees for 10 to 15 minutes.

NOTE TO COOK: Carry to party either on baking sheets or in container. Bake and serve warm.

Try to buy phyllo that has never been frozen; it is easier to work with. If you can find handmade phyllo, it is the best of all.

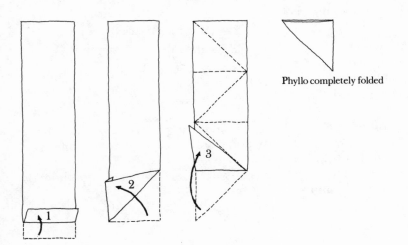

Phyllo completely folded

Marinated lamb Hunan style (F/R3)

3 cups chicken broth or stock
3 cups water
½ cup light soy sauce
½ cup dry or medium-dry sherry
2 cloves star anise
1 cinnamon stick
1 piece dried orange peel 2½ inches by ¼ inch

1-inch piece fresh ginger
2 large cloves garlic, halved
2 tablespoons vegetable oil
6 pounds boned leg of lamb, rolled and tied
1 medium turnip, quartered
2 tablespoons sugar
Fresh parsley for garnish

In large pot combine broth, water, soy sauce, sherry, star anise, cinnamon stick, orange peel, ginger and garlic and bring to boil. Reduce heat; cover and simmer for 15 minutes.

In large skillet(s) heat the oil. Brown the lamb on all sides. Return sauce to boil and add meat. If necessary add boiling water so that sauce comes almost three quarters of the way up the sides of the meat. Return to boil; reduce heat to medium, cover pot and simmer for about 1 hour. From time to time, skim off froth and fat. Add turnip and sugar and simmer until lamb is tender, about another 1½ hours or until meat is easily pierced with fork.

Allow meat to cool in sauce. Refrigerate or freeze. To serve, defrost if frozen and remove layer of fat from top. If refrigerated, remove layer of fat from top. Slice meat thinly and reheat in sauce. Garnish with parsley.

NOTE TO COOK: Carry to party in pot in which the sliced meat will be reheated. Serve on platter with some of sauce poured over. Garnish.

Rice with dried fruits and nuts (F/R2)

9 cups chicken or beef broth or stock
4½ cups long-grain rice
9 tablespoons unsalted butter (1 stick plus 1 tablespoon)
1½ cups whole blanched almonds

2¼ cups dried apricots
2¼ cups pitted dried prunes
2¼ cups raisins or currants
¾ teaspoon cinnamon

Combine broth and rice in large pot and bring to boil over high heat. Stir; reduce heat to simmer and cover pot. Cook about 20 minutes, until rice is tender and liquid has been absorbed.

Melt 1½ tablespoons butter in large skillet over low heat. Add almonds and sauté until golden; remove.

Add remaining butter and melt over medium heat. Stir in fruits and coat and cook until heated through. Mix in almonds and cinnamon and stir in rice.

Refrigerate or freeze, if desired. To reheat, bring to room temperature.

NOTE TO COOK: To carry to party, cook the rice and fruits and combine all ingredients. Carry in heavy-bottomed pan in which the pilaf can be reheated over low heat. Stir often.

Salad of red pepper and celery root (RI)   (12 SERVINGS)

6 red bell peppers

3 large celery roots

6 tablespoons red wine vinegar or balsamic vinegar

3 tablespoons lemon juice

3 tablespoons Dijon mustard

3 teaspoons dried chervil

1½ teaspoons dried tarragon

3 teaspoons finely chopped fresh parsley

¾ cup good-quality olive oil
    Freshly ground black pepper to taste

1½ tablespoons finely chopped fresh parsley for garnish

Wash, core and seed peppers and cut into very fine julienne strips. Julienne celery root with extra-fine julienne blade of food processor (or by hand).

Mix the vinegar, lemon juice, mustard, chervil, tarragon and parsley with a whisk. Gradually whisk in the oil. Season with pepper.

Combine peppers and celery root and pour over dressing, mixing well. Refrigerate at least 4 hours; overnight is fine, too.

NOTE TO COOK: Carry to party in salad bowl tightly wrapped in plastic or in storage container. Carry parsley in plastic bag. Drain off excess dressing and sprinkle with parsley.

This recipe is adapted from one served at Pamela's in Cleveland.

½ pound nitrite-free bacon

3 medium onions, coarsely chopped (about 1¾ cups)

3 cloves garlic, finely minced

4 pounds loose spinach with stems

6 ounces soft goat cheese or 4 ounces farmer cheese and 2 ounces ricotta

Salt and freshly ground pepper to taste

Take 4 pieces of bacon, about 2 inches long, cut into 12 strips and set aside. Cut the remaining bacon into small pieces. Cook the bacon with the onions and garlic over medium-low heat until crisp. When crisp, drain off all the grease, reserving for later use.

Clean spinach by removing tough stems and washing the spinach three times to remove sand. Cook spinach in large pot without additional water until spinach is just wilted. Remove one fourth of the spinach from the pot and place remaining spinach in a colander. Remove all of the liquid from the quarter portion of spinach by placing in a towel and squeezing tightly. There should be about ½ cup. Place this spinach in bowl either with goat cheese or mixture of ricotta and farmer cheese. Blend in food processor or mix thoroughly in bowl. Add bacon mixture; adjust seasoning and stir in 2 tablespoons bacon fat.

Place spinach that is drying in colander onto a towel and lightly remove excess water. Place 12 equal mounds of this spinach on either a wooden board or clean counter. Flatten them each into small rectangles. Season with salt and pepper.

Place 1 tablespoon of spinach-cheese mixture on each bundle and roll up, sealing ends. Do not worry if spinach does not entirely enclose mixture; it doesn't matter.

Place bundles seam side down in baking pan and lay one of the reserved strips of bacon across each widthwise. Refrigerate, if desired. To serve, return to room temperature and bake at 350 degrees 15 to 20 minutes to heat through and crisp bacon strips.

NOTE TO COOK: Carry to party on baking sheet, wrapped in foil and bake. Goat cheese gives much more flavor to dish than farmer cheese.

This is an adaptation of a recipe served at Ventana, a rustic lodge high above California's magnificent Pacific Coastal Highway in Big Sur.

Big Sur is known more for its scenery than its food, with this one exception!

5 eggs	¼ cup sifted cornstarch
1 cup sugar	½ teaspoon vanilla extract
1 cup melted unsalted butter	3 tablespoons orange liqueur
3 ounces semisweet chocolate	Ground nuts, optional
3 ounces unsweetened chocolate	

GLAZE:

6½ ounces semisweet chocolate	⅓ cup heavy cream
2 tablespoons unsalted butter	

Over hot water, in top of double boiler, beat the eggs and sugar until mixture is very light and almost white in color. Remove from heat. Meanwhile, melt the butter and skim off the foam. Return to heat and melt the chocolates. Beat the sifted cornstarch slowly into the egg mixture on low speed until thoroughly blended. Stir the vanilla and orange liqueur into the chocolate mixture and then into the egg mixture. Spoon into a 10-inch springform that has been greased and floured. Bake at 325 degrees for about 20 to 25 minutes, until torte pulls away from sides of pan. Knife inserted in center will not come out clean. Do not overbake. Cool in springform. Remove ring.

To make the glaze, melt chocolate and butter with the cream and spoon over cooled torte. Refrigerate and chill completely. Freeze, well wrapped, if desired. If frozen, defrost, and serve with chill taken off.

If desired, decorate sides with ground almonds, pistachios or hazelnuts, after defrosting.

NOTE TO COOK: Carry to party on serving plate with a tent of aluminum foil.

Mollie's guacamole tostadas

Orange-flavored beef

Piquant crab and olive pasta salad

Salad in a sandwich

Mandarin chicken salad

Lemon ginger cookies

Plum sherbet

No last-minute cooking   Silverware needed: forks, spoons

The eighth person can bring the wine.

This is a recipe adapted from one that Mollie Dickenson brought to our house in Bethesda for a cooperative dinner. It disappeared within minutes.

1 cup dried pinto beans
¾ cup chopped onion
1 large clove garlic, pressed
1½ teaspoons ground cumin
2½ tablespoons mild chile powder
1 tablespoon white vinegar
¼ cup unsalted butter, softened
3 ounces tomato paste
¼ teaspoon ground coriander seed
8 drops hot pepper sauce
Salt and freshly ground black pepper to taste

2 ripe avocados
2 tablespoons lemon juice
1 cup sour cream
2 chopped large tomatoes
¾ cup chopped scallions
1 cup pitted chopped ripe olives
2 cups coarsely grated sharp white cheddar cheese
⅔ cup coarsely chopped fresh coriander (cilantro or Chinese parsley)
Good-quality tortilla chips

To prepare beans either cover with water and soak overnight, or cover with water and bring to boil; boil 2 minutes and allow to sit in water for 1 hour. After soaking beans drain off soaking water. Cover beans with fresh water and cover pot. Bring to boil. Add ½ cup chopped onion, garlic, ½ teaspoon cumin. Cover and simmer until beans are tender, about an hour. Drain.

Place in food processor with ¾ teaspoon cumin, 1½ tablespoons chile powder, vinegar, butter, tomato paste, coriander and hot pepper sauce. Process until mixture is smooth. Adjust seasoning and add salt and pepper to taste.

Peel avocados and mash coarsely with lemon juice and salt and pepper to taste.

Mix sour cream with 1 tablespoon chile powder, ¼ teaspoon cumin.

Chop tomatoes.

Place a layer of the bean mixture in shallow serving dish. Top with mashed avocados then with sour cream mixture. Sprinkle tomatoes evenly over sour cream; sprinkle on scallions, olives and cheese and top with coriander.

Serve with tortilla chips.

NOTE TO COOK: Cook beans a day or two ahead and mix with seasonings. Prepare remaining ingredients except for avocado the day the dish will be served, at your convenience. Just before leaving for party, mash avocados and mix with lemon juice, salt and pepper to taste. Layer salad in serving dish and cover with plastic wrap. Carry to party with tortilla chips in plastic bag.

Orange-flavored beef (R1) (16 SERVINGS)

5 teaspoons dry sherry

2 oval-shaped slices fresh ginger, each about 1 inch long

2 large scallions, each cut into 2 or 3 pieces

4 teaspoons mushroom soy sauce*

1¼ pounds flank steak, thinly sliced and cut into 1-inch squares†

1¼ cups vegetable oil

32 ½-inch squares orange peel

5 dried hot peppers (each about 3 inches long) with seeds, finely chopped

½ cup plus 2 tablespoons chicken broth or stock

Pinch sugar

1¼ teaspoons sesame oil

Combine 2½ teaspoons sherry, ginger, scallions, and 2½ teaspoons soy sauce. Marinate beef in mixture for 10 minutes. Heat oil in wok or large skillet until very hot. Remove ginger and scallions from meat mixture and reserve. Brown beef in oil, stirring constantly for 2 to 3 minutes. Remove beef and drain well on absorbent paper towels. Pour oil out, leaving 1 tablespoon. Add ginger, scallions, orange peel and peppers; stir-fry 1 minute. Add beef, broth and 1½ teaspoons soy sauce, 2½ teaspoons sherry and pinch sugar. Bring to boil; cook rapidly over high heat, stirring until liquid evaporates, 3 to 4 minutes. Sprinkle with sesame oil and serve at room temperature.

NOTE TO COOK: Carry to party in storage container or in serving dish. Provide toothpicks.

Piquant crab and olive pasta salad (R1) (16 SERVINGS)

1½ pounds mixed yellow and green fettucine, fresh if possible

2 (2 ounces drained weight) jars pimiento-stuffed olives, chopped

1 cup Greek (calamata) olives, drained and pitted

2 large cloves garlic, minced

½ cup minced fresh parsley

1 cup homemade mayonnaise (made with part olive oil)

1 cup plain yogurt

6 tablespoons white wine vinegar

3½ tablespoons good-quality olive oil

2 pounds backfin crabmeat

2 ripe avocados, cubed

* If you do not want to buy mushroom soy sauce, available at Oriental grocery stores, use light soy sauce.
† To cut flank steak thinly, freeze for about 1 hour.

Cook fresh fettucine in boiling water about 30 seconds after water has returned to boil. If dried pasta is used, follow package directions, drain and rinse under cold water; drain again.

Combine stuffed green and calamata olives with garlic, parsley, mayonnaise and yogurt. Whisk vinegar with oil and combine with mayonnaise mixture. Gently stir in crabmeat and add fettucine to crab mixture. Refrigerate until serving time.

Just before serving, cube avocados and mix in carefully.

NOTE TO COOK: Carry to party in storage container or salad bowl wrapped with plastic. Carry avocados separately. Add avocado to salad just before serving.

Salad in a sandwich (R1)   (16 SERVINGS)

2 pounds zucchini, scrubbed, ends cut off and cut into julienne strips, about 1 inch long, ¼-inch thick	½ cup freshly squeezed lemon juice
2 large green peppers, cut into julienne strips, about 1 inch long, ¼-inch thick	9 tablespoons good-quality olive oil
	2 tablespoons white wine vinegar
	3 teaspoons anchovy paste
2 cups coarsely shredded Muenster cheese	2 tablespoons chopped fresh thyme or 2 teaspoons dried thyme leaves
1 cup minced fresh parsley	
2 tablespoons capers	Freshly ground black pepper to taste
8 large scallions, thinly sliced	16 small whole-wheat pitas

Combine zucchini, peppers, cheese, parsley, capers and scallions and mix gently. Beat the lemon juice with the oil and vinegar. Then beat in anchovy paste, thyme and pepper.

Vegetable-cheese mixture and dressing may be prepared ahead and refrigerated separately.

When ready to serve, toss vegetables with dressing and sprinkle with additional pepper. Slice off enough of the top of each pita so that the salad may be spooned in. Toast pitas.

NOTE TO COOK: Toss vegetables with dressing at home and carry to party in storage container or serving bowl. Carry pitas to party separately. Just before serving, toast pitas.

Let people make their own sandwiches. Serve leftover salad on side.

Mandarin chicken salad

4 large chicken breasts

½ cup creamy-style peanut butter

½ cup water

½ cup light soy sauce

6 tablespoons white vinegar

¼ cup Oriental sesame oil*

¼ cup dry white wine

2 tablespoons sugar

¾ cup thinly sliced scallions

2 tablespoons very finely slivered pickled red ginger*

4 to 6 cups peanut oil

8 ounces rice noodles, broken into 3-inch lengths

8 cups finely shredded curly leaf lettuce

5 teaspoons black sesame seeds*

Poach chicken breasts in simmering water to cover until they are no longer pink in the center, 10 to 15 minutes. Drain; set aside to cool. When cool enough to handle, remove skin and bones and cut into fine shreds.

Stir water into peanut butter and stir until smooth. Add soy sauce, vinegar, sesame oil, wine, sugar; stir in 2 tablespoons of the scallions and the red ginger.

Heat some of the peanut oil in a large saucepan over medium-high heat to 400 degrees on a deep-frying thermometer. Add a handful of noodles; cook until noodles puff up and turn golden, just a few seconds. Immediately remove with slotted spoon or tongs and drain on absorbent paper towels. Repeat with remaining noodles in handfuls until all of them are cooked. Add oil as needed and bring oil up to proper heat before adding more noodles.

To prepare ahead, chicken may be poached a day ahead and refrigerated. Sauce may be prepared a day ahead and refrigerated.

Return chicken and sauce to room temperature before using. Noodles may be prepared earlier in the day and kept at room temperature until serving.

To serve, arrange a bed of lettuce on large platter or platters. Gently toss rice noodles and chicken with sauce and arrange on lettuce bed. Sprinkle with remaining scallions and black sesame seeds.

NOTE TO COOK: Carry noodles to party in large plastic bag(s) or in bowl. Carry chicken, scallions, sesame seeds and lettuce in separate plastic bags. Carry sauce in container with tight-fitting lid.

Arrange at party in large serving bowl.

* These items are available at Oriental grocery stores.

For a magazine story I had to round up the best cookies across the United States. These came from Jill Heavenrich of Nashota Ovens in Milwaukee.

2½ cups sifted unbleached flour
 2 teaspoons baking soda
 ½ teaspoon salt (optional)
 3 teaspoons ground ginger
 1 teaspoon ground cinnamon
 ¾ cup unsalted butter, softened

1 cup firmly packed dark brown sugar
1 egg
¼ cup unsulphured molasses
1 tablespoon grated lemon rind
¼ cup granulated sugar

Sift together flour, baking soda, salt, ginger and cinnamon onto waxed paper.

Beat butter with brown sugar and egg in large bowl until light and fluffy. Beat in molasses and lemon rind until well blended. Stir in dry ingredients, half at a time, blending well after each addition.

Roll dough into balls, 1 level tablespoon at a time, between palms of hands; roll in granulated sugar. Place balls 2 inches apart on ungreased cookie sheets.

Bake at 350 degrees for 10 minutes. Do not overbake. Cookies will be soft in the center. Cool completely on wire racks and store in tightly covered containers.

NOTE TO COOK: Carry to party in covered container and arrange on serving dish.

8 cups whole ripe red plums,
  about 28
2 3-inch sticks cinnamon
¾ cup fresh lemon juice

Grated rinds of 4 lemons
4 cups sugar
6 cups buttermilk

Put plums and cinnamon sticks in large pan(s) with 2 cups water. Cover and simmer gently for 10 minutes. Cool enough so you can handle the plums. Pit and puree them in food processor or blender. You will need about 4 cups puree. If all the skin does not puree, that's fine. It adds texture and color to the sherbet. Drain off liquid. Return puree to pan with cinnamon sticks, sugar, lemon juice and rind. Simmer until sugar is dissolved. Remove cinnamon sticks. Cool and add buttermilk. Mix well and pour into shallow trays for freezing. Freeze until almost firm. Remove sherbet from trays and place in chilled bowl; beat until smooth. Return to trays and freeze until firm. Use within a few days.

Very tart and tangy and very refreshing.

NOTE TO COOK: Carry to party in insulated containers. To serve, place in large bowl.

Sesame toasts
New Mexican cheese spread

Basil, chicken and potatoes
Black-eyed pea and ham salad
Marinated mushrooms and cherry tomatoes

Poppy seed dressing for summer fruits
Chocolate chunk cookies

All cold   Silverware needed: forks

One person can cut up the fruit, another make the dressing. A third can bring the wine, another soft drinks or hard liquor.

This is a very simple menu with the minimum of last-minute effort.

Sesame toasts (R7)   (ABOUT 5 DOZEN)

8-ounce loaf Italian or French bread, about 2 inches in diameter

¾ cup unsalted butter

2 teaspoons Oriental sesame oil

2 eggs, beaten lightly

¾ cup sesame seeds

Cut loaf crosswise at slight angle into ¼-inch-thick slices. Melt butter with sesame oil. Brush both sides of each slice with some of butter mixture; brush one side of each slice with egg and dip that side into sesame seeds.

Arrange slices, sesame side up, on baking sheets and bake at 375 degrees for 20 to 25 minutes, until toasts are golden and crisp.

Toasts can be stored in airtight container for a week at room temperature.

NOTE TO COOK: Carry to party in storage container. Arrange on serving tray.

New Mexican cheese spread (RI)

16 ounces cream cheese, softened

1½ cups sharp white cheddar cheese, finely grated

1 medium avocado, mashed

1 small onion, finely minced

1 clove garlic, minced

3- or 4-ounce can chopped green chiles

Crackers

Blend cheeses together. Add remaining ingredients and mix well. Or add all ingredients to food processor and blend well with steel blade. Spoon into serving dish and chill. Serve with crackers.

NOTE TO COOK: Carry to party in serving dish covered with plastic. Carry crackers separately.

Basil, chicken and potatoes (RI)

(20 SERVINGS)

4 eggs

½ cup good-quality olive oil

¼ cup lemon juice

4 cups fresh basil leaves, tightly packed

1⅓ cups mayonnaise (homemade preferred)

1 cup plain yogurt

8 cups cubed cooked chicken breast (about 4½ pounds boneless before cooking)

8 cups pared cubed cooked potatoes (about 3 pounds before cooking)

Salt and freshly ground black pepper to taste

Red leaf lettuce for garnish

Combine eggs, ¼ cup oil and lemon juice in food processor or blender and blend. With motor running add remaining oil in thin, steady stream and process until thickened. Add basil and process until pureed. Add mayonnaise and blend. Transfer to bowl and stir in yogurt.

Stir in chicken and potatoes. Season to taste with salt and pepper. Chill, overnight if desired. Serve on bowl lined with red leaf lettuce.

NOTE TO COOK: Carry to party either in storage container or in serving bowl, covered with plastic. If assembling at party, carry lettuce, already washed and drained, in plastic bag.

This recipe has been adapted from one served by Larry Forgione at his restaurant, An American Place, in New York.

1½ pounds black-eyed peas
2 medium onions
2 medium carrots
2 cloves garlic
1¾ pounds nitrite-free Virginia-style or smoked ham, cut into ¼-by-¼-inch pieces

¾ cup chopped fresh parsley
1 teaspoon hot pepper sauce
Oil and vinegar dressing
Salt and freshly ground black pepper to taste
1½ cups diced seeded tomatoes

Wash peas and soak for 12 to 24 hours in water to cover; drain. Place soaked peas, onions, carrots and garlic in 6-quart pot. Cover with cold water and bring to boil; lower heat immediately and simmer until peas are tender, 45 to 60 minutes. Remove onions, carrots and garlic and set aside. Drain peas, discarding any visible shells.

Cut onions and carrots into fine dice; mash or finely chop garlic. Mix these ingredients with the drained peas. Add the ham, parsley, hot pepper sauce and dressing and season with salt and pepper. Stir gently to distribute dressing. Refrigerate until well chilled, overnight if desired. When ready to serve, stir in diced tomatoes gently.

OIL AND VINEGAR DRESSING:

½ cup good-quality olive oil
6 tablespoons vegetable oil
½ cup red wine vinegar
3 tablespoons lemon juice
2½ teaspoons Japanese or imported Chinese soy sauce
½ teaspoon Worcestershire sauce
1 teaspoon sugar

2 tablespoons whole-grain mustard
4 cloves garlic, sliced
1½ tablespoons fresh basil, chopped, or 1 teaspoon dried basil
1½ teaspoons dried oregano

Mix all ingredients together with whisk and pour over salad.

NOTE TO COOK: Carry salad to party in storage container or in salad bowl tightly covered with plastic. Carry tomatoes either whole or diced in plastic bag or container. Mix tomatoes in with salad just before serving.

Marinated mushrooms and cherry tomatoes (R3) (20 SERVINGS)

3 cups good-quality olive oil

½ cup plus 2 tablespoons red wine vinegar

Freshly ground black pepper and salt to taste

3 large cloves garlic, finely chopped

1½ tablespoons dried basil or 4½ tablespoons fresh basil, chopped

1 teaspoon dried thyme leaves

6 tablespoons coarsely chopped fresh parsley

3 pounds small to medium mushrooms

4 pint baskets cherry tomatoes, washed and stemmed

Combine all ingredients but mushrooms and tomatoes. Whisk. Wash and dry mushrooms, cutting off ends of the stems. Gently stir mushrooms into marinade. Cover and refrigerate for at least 1 day, up to 3. Add the tomatoes 24 hours before serving, but no longer. Stir occasionally to be sure the vegetables on top are covered by the marinade. Keep under the marinade with crushed waxed paper, if necessary.

To serve, drain and place in serving bowl.

NOTE TO COOK: Bring to party in storage container and drain and place in serving bowl at party.

Poppy seed dressing for summer fruits (R1)   (20 SERVINGS)

1 tablespoon grated orange peel

2 cups plain yogurt

2 tablespoons plus 2 teaspoons raspberry vinegar

2 tablespoons plus 2 teaspoons frozen orange juice concentrate, defrosted, undiluted

2 tablespoons plus 2 teaspoons Grand Marnier

2 tablespoons plus 2 teaspoons toasted poppy seeds

24 cups mixed fresh fruits, cut up

Mix together all ingredients but fruit and refrigerate. To serve, cut up fruit and serve dressing on the side.

NOTE TO COOK: Carry dressing to party in storage container. Carry fruit to party, cut up, in storage container. Serve dressing in sauceboat with ladle. Serve fruit in large bowl.

1½ cups firmly packed dark brown sugar

1 cup unsalted butter

1 teaspoon vanilla extract

Dash salt

2 cups unbleached flour

1½ cups coarsely ground pecans, about 6 ounces*

8 ounces good-quality sweet eating chocolate

Beat brown sugar and butter until creamy. Beat in vanilla, salt, flour and pecans and blend well. Break up bars of chocolate into irregular pieces, none of which should be larger than about ¼ inch. Stir in chocolate.

Drop from heaping tablespoon onto greased cookie sheets, leaving about 2 inches between them to spread out. Bake at 325 degrees 6 to 8 minutes. Do not overbake or the cookies will harden. They should have soft, chewy centers.

NOTE TO COOK: Carry to party in container and arrange on serving dish.

* You can get the desired texture for the pecans by putting them into a food processor with the steel blade and processing until some of the mixture is finely ground but most is coarsely ground, like a very finely chopped mixture.

Three cheese pie

Portuguese pork and clams
Soy-marinated skirt steaks
Carrots with coriander
Cold broccoli with yogurt-ginger dressing
Tortilla de patata

Pears poached in red wine with basil
Tuiles

Cooking facilities needed: top of the stove   *Silverware needed: forks, spoons*

This is the kind of cooperative dinner that can be very informal or very fancy. The meal is suitable for both kinds of parties. It can be a stand-up buffet, a sit-down buffet or a sit-down dinner.

Three cheese pie (R3)   (18 TO 20 SERVINGS)

1 pound sweet Gorgonzola, softened

¾ cup plus ½ cup chopped walnuts

8 ounces mascarpone or whipped cream cheese, softened

¼ pound unsalted butter, softened

1 pound ricotta

⅓ cup pignoli nuts

4 tablespoons slivered almonds
   Italian or French bread

Cut a round of waxed paper to fit the bottom of a 5- or 6-inch diameter soufflé dish. Spread two thirds of the Gorgonzola in a smooth layer in bottom of dish. Top with ¾ cup walnuts; press into cheese. Smooth on a layer of mascarpone. Smooth on a layer of butter. Sprinkle on remaining walnuts; press in. Smooth on a layer of remaining Gorgonzola. Top with layer of ricotta. Cover and chill at least overnight.

To unmold, dip the dish briefly in hot water; run knife around the edge and unmold. Remove waxed paper. Then reverse pie onto serving dish. Decorate top and sides with pignoli and almonds. Allow to sit at room temperature for 30 minutes before serving. Slice very thinly with a very sharp knife. Serve with Italian or French bread, thinly cut.

NOTE TO COOK: Carry to party in soufflé dish, well wrapped. Carry pignoli and almonds in separate plastic bags. Carry sliced bread in foil or plastic bag. Unmold and decorate the pie at party.

Portuguese pork and clams (R2) (16 SERVINGS)

Jim Beard had this at my house the first time I made it. I wasn't too pleased with the results: too dry, tough clams. Not enough flavor. He suggested cooking the clams separately and adding mussels for a nice contrast. He also thought adding some cumin would be a good idea.

This version of a very well-known Portuguese dish is the result.

6 cups dry white wine

3 tablespoons plus 1 teaspoon Hungarian sweet paprika

Freshly ground black pepper and salt to taste

6 medium cloves garlic, minced

6 small bay leaves

6 pounds lean boneless pork, cut in ½-inch cubes (use pork loin)

½ cup vegetable oil

6 onions, sliced

4 ripe tomatoes, seeded and chopped

6 large cloves garlic, pressed

2 2-inch dried red chiles, seeds removed and broken up

1 tablespoon ground cumin

48 small clams (cherrystones) and mussels, soaked and scrubbed

⅔ cup minced fresh coriander

½ cup fresh chopped parsley

2 lemons, cut in 16 wedges

Combine wine, paprika, salt, pepper, 6 cloves minced garlic, bay leaves and mix well. Add pork and marinate in the mixture for 8 hours or overnight. Mix occasionally.

Drain pork and reserve marinade, discarding bay leaves. Heat oil in large skillet. Sauté onions and pork over high heat in oil until onions are soft and pork browns. Add tomatoes, remaining garlic, chiles, cumin and reserved marinade. Cover and simmer until pork is tender, about 1 hour. This portion of the recipe may be prepared ahead and reheated. To serve, heat pork, steam clams and mussels, about 8 minutes, until shells open. (Discard any shells that do not open.) Spoon pork into serving dish; arrange clams and mussels on top. Sprinkle with coriander and parsley and decorate with lemon wedges.

NOTE TO COOK: Cook pork at home and carry to party in cooking pot. Scrub clams and mussels and carry to party in separate cooking pot. Chop coriander and parsley and cut lemons into wedges. Carry to party in separate plastic bags. At serving time, reheat pork, steam clams and mussels and finish dish.

Soy-marinated skirt steaks

5 large cloves garlic, put through press

3 tablespoons imported Chinese soy sauce or Japanese soy sauce

1½ teaspoons dried oregano leaves

3 tablespoons vegetable oil

3 tablespoons tomato paste

Freshly ground black pepper to taste

3 pounds skirt or flank steaks*

Greens such as parsley or watercress for decoration

Combine the garlic, soy sauce, oregano, oil, tomato paste and pepper and spread on both sides of steaks. Refrigerate overnight.

Broil steaks 2 inches from source of heat for 3 to 5 minutes on each side. Slice very thinly on the diagonal and serve at room temperature.

NOTE TO COOK: Prepare steaks at home within an hour of going to the party. Do not refrigerate. Carry to party on serving platter, well wrapped. Decorate platter with greens and serve.

* If flank steaks are used, score each side lightly before spreading with marinade.

Carrots with coriander

4 pounds young carrots

2 teaspoons ground coriander seed

½ cup dry sherry

Freshly ground black pepper to taste

4 to 6 tablespoons fresh lemon juice

Scrape carrots and slice using regular slicer blade of food processor. Steam slices for 4 to 5 minutes. Combine carrots with coriander and sherry. When ready to serve, heat through. Season with pepper and lemon juice to taste.

NOTE TO COOK: Steam carrots and mix with coriander and sherry at home, if desired, within an hour or two of going to party. Carry to party in plastic container with tight-fitting lid. Carry remaining ingredients separately. At party heat carrots and season with pepper and lemon juice just before serving.

Cold broccoli with yogurt-ginger dressing

(Dressing R2)

16 medium stalks broccoli
3 cups plain yogurt
2 tablespoons light soy sauce

2 tablespoons finely minced fresh ginger
3 large cloves garlic, minced

Cut off stems of broccoli; set aside for another use such as soup. Divide tops of broccoli into florets. Steam the florets for 5 to 7 minutes, until crisp-tender. Rinse under cold water and chill for an hour or several hours.

Combine yogurt with remaining ingredients and refrigerate.

To serve, arrange broccoli on shallow serving plate and pour yogurt dressing over.

NOTE TO COOK: Carry broccoli and dressing separately to party and combine at party.

Tortilla de patata (potato omelet)

(16 SERVINGS)

In Spain this dish is eaten at room temperature, intensifying the flavors.

1 cup (approximately) vegetable oil (preferably combination of olive and corn oils)
3 large onions, finely chopped
15 cups peeled, thinly sliced potatoes
3 small green peppers, diced

3 cloves garlic, minced
Salt and freshly ground black pepper to taste
1 teaspoon cayenne
1½ dozen large eggs, lightly beaten

Heat ¼ cup mixture of oils in each of 2 12-inch skillets. Add ½ of onions, potatoes, green peppers, garlic, salt and pepper to each skillet. Cover and cook over medium heat, stirring mixture occasionally to prevent sticking. When potatoes are tender, in about 15 to 20 minutes, but not brown, remove and cool slightly.

Add cooled vegetable mixture to beaten eggs. Clean out one skillet and add 3 tablespoons of remaining oil. Heat and add one half of egg mixture; cook over medium heat until bottom becomes golden brown. With spatula loosen omelet from pan. Place a plate on top of pan and invert. Free skillet of any bits of omelet that may have stuck. Add a bit more oil, if necessary. Slide omelet back into skillet and cook second side until golden. Repeat with remaining oil and egg mixture. Cut into wedges and serve at room temperature.

NOTE TO COOK: Make omelets at home up to 3 hours ahead and cut into wedges. Do not refrigerate. Carry to party on serving dish, well wrapped with foil or plastic. Do not wrap tightly if omelets are still warm. Just cover.

Pears poached in red wine with basil (R1)

16 firm ripe pears, with stems	2½ cups sugar
8 cups water	3 branches fresh rosemary or
Juice of 1 large lemon	2½ teaspoons dry rosemary
5½ cups dry red wine	

Peel pears and slice off a bit of the bottom so that pears can stand up. Place peeled pears in mixture of water and lemon juice as they are peeled.

Mix the wine and sugar with rosemary and boil for 5 minutes. Add pears and simmer, covered until they are tender. (That will depend on how ripe they are.) Baste often while pears are simmering. Remove pears, boil syrup to reduce slightly and pour hot syrup over pears. Serve at room temperature or chilled.

NOTE TO COOK: Prepare pears and carry to party in tightly covered plastic container. Arrange on serving dish at party.

Tuiles (R2)

(4 DOZEN)

3 egg whites	5 tablespoons melted butter
1 cup plus 3 tablespoons confectioners' sugar	½ teaspoon vanilla extract
1½ cups sliced almonds	½ teaspoon almond extract
Scant ½ cup cake flour	

Beat whites until frothy; add sugar and mix well. Combine flour and almonds and add to egg-white mixture; mix well. Fold in butter, vanilla and almond extracts.

Drop by heaping teaspoonfuls onto lightly buttered cookie sheets. With moist fork, flatten to make round shapes.

Bake at 325 degrees for 9 to 11 minutes or until golden. As soon as the cookies are removed from the oven, shape around a small glass to form tiles like those found on the roof of a French house ("tuiles" means tiles).

Oven-fried potato peelings
Frittatas

Cold Oriental noodles

Middle Eastern chicken with bulgur
Hot cherry tomatoes vinaigrette

Mushroom and fennel salad with cheeses*
and bread

Mocha almond cakes

Cooking facilities needed: oven and top of stove   Silverware needed: forks, knives

This is one of those large, fairly elaborate parties at which you can either divide the work among all the guests, asking three different ones, for instance, to bring one cake (you will need three cakes) and have two people make the chicken. Someone else can bring the wine, someone else the champagne, someone else the flowers, because this is the perfect kind of party for a very special occasion. Or it can be cooked by just a few of the guests. It is the menu served at my house last year in honor of a birthday. Most people have no place to seat thirty, but many can manage to find seats all over the house for that number. With this dinner you need to sit down. It has four courses in addition to the hors d'oeuvres.

Too big for your plans? Just do it for ten and divide every recipe in thirds.

It involves some last-minute cooking and preparation.

* Three or four cheeses served with very thinly sliced French or Italian bread or melba toast. You might like to use a well-flavored goat cheese, sweet Gorgonzola, taleggio or French triple crème. You will need to buy more cheese than is necessary so that the pieces look nice on the cheese tray. Allow about two slices of bread per person.

215

Oven-fried potato peelings (Sauce R2; Potatoes R1)   (ABOUT 6 DOZEN)

9 scrubbed baking potatoes

6 tablespoons unsalted butter, melted

2 medium cloves garlic, minced

SAUCE:

1 cup plain yogurt, drained of visible whey

¾ teaspoon chopped fresh rosemary

Freshly ground black pepper to taste

½ teaspoon chopped fresh rosemary

Bake potatoes at 400 degrees 50 to 60 minutes, until done. Cut in half and scoop out most of potatoes (reserve for another use). Cut skins in strips ½ inch wide.

Combine butter, garlic, rosemary and pepper. Dip inside of strips in butter mixture and arrange skin side down in single layer on baking sheet. Refrigerate if desired. Return to room temperature before baking. Bake peelings at 450 degrees until they are browned, 15 to 20 minutes; turn and bake another 10 or 15 minutes until they are crisp. Transfer to absorbent paper towels and drain.

For the sauce, mix the yogurt with the rosemary.

Serve the warm potato skin strips with yogurt sauce for dipping.

NOTE TO COOK: Prepare potatoes as much as a day ahead except for baking. Prepare sauce a day or two ahead.

Carry sauce to party in serving dish tightly wrapped with plastic or in container with tight-fitting lid. Carry potatoes to party on baking sheets wrapped in foil and bake as directed.

Frittatas (F/R1)   (MAKES 60)

1½ 10-ounce packages frozen chopped spinach

3 cups ricotta cheese

2¼ cups finely grated fresh Parmesan cheese

1¾ cups finely chopped fresh mushrooms or black olives

6 tablespoons finely chopped onion

1½ teaspoons dried oregano leaves or 1½ tablespoons chopped fresh oregano

2 eggs

Thaw spinach and squeeze dry. Mix with remaining ingredients. Lightly grease miniature muffin cups (approximately 1-inch diameter). Spoon in mixture. Refrigerate if desired.

To serve, bake at 375 degrees for about 25 minutes, until mixture is firm and golden. Cool 10 minutes and serve warm.

These may be frozen after baking. To reheat, place frozen frittatas on baking sheets and bake at 375 degrees for about 10 minutes, until they are heated completely.

NOTE TO COOK: Either bake at home and reheat at party at 375, for 10 minutes if frozen, for 5 minutes if not. Or prepare and spoon into muffin tins and bake at party as directed.

Cold Oriental noodles (R4)   (30 SERVINGS)

3 pounds fresh Chinese egg noodles, ¹⁄₁₆ inch thick, or comparable Italian or American egg noodles

½ cup plus 2 tablespoons sesame oil

7½ tablespoons light Chinese soy sauce or Japanese soy sauce

4½ tablespoons balsamic or rice vinegar

6 tablespoons sugar

2 to 3 tablespoons hot chili oil

3-inch piece fresh ginger, minced

¾ to 1 cup thinly sliced scallions

Additional scallions, thinly sliced for garnish

Cook fresh noodles in boiling water for 2 to 3 minutes. If noodles are dried, follow package directions. Chill immediately under cold running water.

Blend remaining ingredients except garnish and stir gently into noodles. Refrigerate at least 1 day for best flavor.

To serve, stir noodles and sprinkle with scallion.

NOTE TO COOK: Carry to party either in storage container or in serving bowl, depending on whether guests will help themselves to noodles or noodles will be served on individual plates. Either way, carry the garnish separately and add it at serving time.

BULGUR:

1 cup unsalted butter	28 large prunes, quartered
5 medium onions, diced	1 cup pine nuts
7 stalks celery, diced	Freshly ground black pepper and salt to taste
7 cups bulgur	
7 cups chicken broth or stock	

Melt butter in one or more large saucepans and sauté onion and celery over medium-high heat until onion is translucent. Add bulgur; reduce heat and cook until bulgur is coated and beginning to color. Stir in chicken broth and bring to boil. Reduce heat to low and cook, covered, until liquid is absorbed, about 10 minutes. Add prunes and pine nuts to mixture and season with salt and pepper.

CHICKEN:

21 whole chicken breasts, skinned, boned and halved	Juice of 14 large lemons
Freshly ground black pepper and salt to taste	42 prunes
1¾ cups vegetable oil	1¾ to 2¼ cups honey
Juice of 14 large oranges	¼ to ½ teaspoon cayenne
	Orange slices for garnish

While bulgur is cooking, pound chicken breasts to ¼-inch thickness. Season with pepper and salt. Heat enough oil in one or more large skillets to film pans (allow about 1 tablespoon of oil per breast half). Sauté breasts and brown on both sides. Remove from pan and repeat until all are done. Set aside. Add orange and lemon juices, prunes, honey and cayenne to pan. Season again with pepper and salt.

Cook juices over medium-high heat to reduce slightly and thicken a little. Spoon bulgur into pans to make thin, even layers. Top with chicken breasts; cover and cook until chicken is thoroughly heated. Garnish with orange slices.

To prepare ahead, complete recipe to the point where all the ingredients are in the pans together, but instead of putting them in the pans, place them in large containers that can be stored in the freezer or refrigerator. If freezing, make sure the chicken is covered by the sauce.

To serve, return to room temperature. Cook in large skillets until chicken is heated all the way through and bulgur and sauce are bubbling. Arrange on serving platters and decorate with orange slices.

NOTE TO COOK: Carry to party in storage containers (if hostess does not have enough large skillets for cooking that many chicken breasts, you may have to bring your own) and finish cooking at party.

5 pints cherry tomatoes, stemmed and washed

3⅓ cups fresh parsley leaves

15 scallions, cut into 1-inch lengths

5 ribs celery, cut into 1-inch pieces

½ cup plus 2 tablespoons vegetable oil

6 tablespoons plus 2 teaspoons red wine vinegar

4 scant teaspoons dried oregano

Freshly ground black pepper to taste

Place the tomatoes in baking dish that will hold them in a single layer (or use two dishes).

Mince the parsley in food processor. Add scallions and celery and pulse food processor just until celery is minced. Add remaining ingredients and process long enough to mix, just a few seconds.

Pour over tomatoes and refrigerate, if desired. To serve, return tomatoes to room temperature and bake at 500 degrees for 10 minutes. Watch so that tomatoes do not burst.

NOTE TO COOK: Prepare tomatoes and carry to party in baking dish(es) wrapped in aluminum foil. Bake at party.

Mushroom and fennel salad (R1)   (30 SERVINGS)

5 pounds large mushrooms, sliced

5 cups fennel, cut into julienne strips*

10 red bell peppers, diced

2 cups less 2 tablespoons good-quality olive oil

5 cloves garlic, minced

1 cup plus 1½ tablespoons red wine vinegar

5 teaspoons fennel seeds

5 bay leaves, crushed

Freshly ground black pepper to taste

Combine mushrooms, fennel and red pepper in large bowl or bowls. In separate bowl whisk oil, garlic and vinegar. Whisk in fennel seeds, bay leaves and pepper. Pour over vegetables and toss well. Cover and refrigerate overnight, if desired, but at least 4 hours. To serve, stir and pour off excess dressing.

NOTE TO COOK: Carry to party in storage container or serving bowl. Stir well before serving and pour off excess dressing.

The salad is accompanied by cheeses and bread, brought by another guest.

* If fresh fennel is unavailable, celery may be substituted, but the taste is entirely different.

Mocha almond cakes (F/RI)

This is a special-occasion cake, particularly suited for a birthday party. (Make 3.)

CAKE:

1 pound unsalted butter
2 cups sugar
1¾ cups unbleached flour
1 cup blanched ground almonds
2 teaspoons baking powder

8 eggs, separated
2 teaspoons almond extract
Rinds of 2 large oranges
Rind of 1 large lemon

Cream butter to consistency of mayonnaise. Add sugar slowly, continuing to beat. Beat until light and fluffy. Combine flour, almonds and baking powder. Beat egg yolks into butter mixture one at a time, alternating with flour mixture. Beat in almond extract and rinds of oranges and lemon.

Beat egg whites until stiff but not dry; fold into cake batter. Spoon batter into well-greased 9-inch springform and bake approximately 1¾ hours at 325 degrees, or until cake tests done. Cool in pan 10 minutes. Loosen cake and invert on cake rack. Cool completely. Cut cake into 4 equal rounds. Fill and frost.

FILLING:

¾ pound unsalted butter
1½ cups confectioners' sugar
5 egg yolks
1 tablespoon hot water mixed with 1 tablespoon instant coffee

20-ounce jar good-quality tart apricot jam
1 to 2 tablespoons lemon juice
3 tablespoons Grand Marnier or other orange liqueur

Cream butter until almost white; add sugar and yolks one at a time, beating after each addition. Add coffee mixture; beat well and set aside.

Mix jam with lemon juice to desired tartness and mix in Grand Marnier.

Spread half of the jam mixture on bottom layer of cake. Top with second layer and spread with half of buttercream mixture. Top with third layer and cover with remaining jam. Top with fourth layer and cover top and sides with remaining buttercream mixture.

Freeze or refrigerate, if desired. If frozen, defrost to serve.

NOTE TO COOK: For a party for thirty people you will need to make three cakes. The cakes must be made separately, but the filling and frosting for all three can be made at once.

Carry to party carefully wrapped in aluminum foil.

FALL—WINTER DINNER FOR 16 OR 18

Bon bon chicken

Cheddar-cumin toast

Transylvanian cabbage

Apple-barley pilaf

Orange and red onion salad

Carrie Lee's vermicelli

Ginger cheesecake

Black and white cheesecake

Cooking facilities needed: top of stove and oven   *Silverware needed: forks*

Ask the noncook to bring the wine.
This is a very hearty meal.

Bon bon chicken (R1) (18 SERVINGS)

¾ of an 8-ounce jar Oriental sesame paste*

½ teaspoon chopped fresh ginger

1 clove garlic, minced

1½ teaspoons Chinese chile sauce or chile paste*

6 tablespoons water

2 teaspoons sugar

3 tablespoons white vinegar

3 tablespoons light Chinese soy sauce or Japanese soy sauce

9 chicken breast halves

5 medium cucumbers, peeled, seeded and cut into julienne strips

Chopped unsalted peanuts for garnish

Stir the separated oil into the sesame paste to mix well. Combine the paste with ginger, garlic, chile, water, sugar, vinegar and soy sauce. Blend well in blender or beat with fork.

Bring 6 cups of water to boil; add chicken breasts and return water to boil. Reduce heat to simmer; cook for 5 minutes, turn off heat and let chicken cool in liquid. Remove bones and skin. Shred chicken meat with your fingers.

To serve, arrange cucumbers on large platter; top with shredded chicken. Pour sauce over chicken and cucumbers and serve at room temperature. Sprinkle with chopped peanuts. Or refrigerate cooked chicken, if desired. Refrigerate cucumber sticks. To serve, return ingredients to room temperature and follow directions for serving.

Small plates and forks are needed for this hors d'oeuvre.

NOTE TO COOK: Carry chicken, cucumbers, sauce and peanuts in separate containers to party. Arrange at party as directed.

Cheddar-cumin toast (R7) (MAKES ½-CUP SPREAD)

3 cups coarsely grated, unpacked white cheddar cheese

3 tablespoons coarsely chopped, pitted green Greek olives (or other very flavorful olives)

3 large thinly sliced scallions

3 tablespoons mayonnaise

1½ teaspoons ground cumin

½ teaspoon ground ginger, scant

3 or 4 dashes cayenne

Thinly sliced French bread (ficelle size or larger), about 40 slices

* Available at Oriental markets. If you cannot find Oriental sesame paste, you can substitute creamy peanut butter.

Thoroughly combine all the ingredients but the bread. Refrigerate, if desired. To serve, spread on thin slices of French bread and broil for 2 or 3 minutes, until cheese melts and begins to color. Watch carefully. Serve warm.

NOTE TO COOK: Spread bread with mixture at home. Carry prepared slices to party and broil before or after potato peelings are ready. Arrange on serving tray.

Transylvanian cabbage gulyás (goulash) (RI) (16–18 SERVINGS)

A wonderfully rich and hearty Hungarian dish.

3 cloves garlic, minced

3 medium to large onions, finely chopped

2 small green peppers, cut into strips

5 tablespoons vegetable oil

5 slices nitrite-free bacon, diced

3 tablespoons sweet Hungarian paprika

3 pounds lean, boneless pork, cut into ½-inch cubes

Freshly ground black pepper to taste

1½ teaspoons caraway seeds

3 pounds fresh sauerkraut

1½ pounds smoked sausage or bratwurst

16 ounces sour cream

In a large pot sauté the garlic, onions and peppers in hot oil and bacon for 5 minutes, over low heat, stirring frequently, until onions are light golden. Remove pot from heat and add paprika. Mix well. Add pork cubes and stir to coat. Return to heat and cook over low heat for a few minutes, stirring continuously to make sure the paprika does not burn. Season with pepper and caraway seeds and mix well.

Add enough water to cover meat; cover pot and simmer for 45 minutes.

While meat is cooking, wash sauerkraut under cold running water and squeeze dry. Add sauerkraut to meat and cook another 15 minutes, or until meat is done.

Meanwhile, if using bratwurst, cook in boiling water until done, about 10 minutes. Smoked sausage does not need additional cooking. Slice sausage and add to gulyás.

This dish is best if prepared a day ahead and refrigerated.

To serve, reheat thoroughly; reduce heat to simmer and stir in sour cream. Do not allow to boil or sour cream will separate.

NOTE TO COOK: Prepare gulyás and refrigerate. Carry to party in pot in which it was cooked; carry sour cream in its container. Reheat at party; add sour cream and heat through.

Apple-barley pilaf (R1)

5 tablespoons unsalted butter
3 medium-large onions
2½ cups barley
5 cups chicken broth or stock
1¼ cups raisins

1¼ teaspoons dried thyme leaves, crushed
5 apples, cored and finely chopped
½ cup chopped fresh parsley

Melt butter in large skillet with tight-fitting lid. Add onions and sauté until barely tender. Add barley; cook and stir occasionally over medium heat until barley begins to take on color. Add chicken broth, raisins and thyme. Bring to boil; reduce heat and simmer covered 35 to 45 minutes. Fold in apples and parsley. Heat through. Or refrigerate before cooking barley. To serve, return mixture to boil; reduce heat and simmer until liquid is absorbed—20 to 30 minutes—and barley is tender.

Chop apples and parsley and fold in. Heat through.

NOTE TO COOK: Carry barley to party in pot and cook. Bring chopped parsley in plastic bag. Bring apples whole and chop just before adding to barley; otherwise they will darken.

Orange and red onion salad

8 medium seedless oranges
4 medium red onions
1 cup plus 2 tablespoons dry red wine
6 tablespoons good-quality olive oil
3 tablespoons tarragon vinegar

6 tablespoons chopped onion
4 small cloves garlic, put through press
Freshly ground black pepper to taste
8 dozen pitted black Italian, French or Greek olives, halved

Peel oranges and slice horizontally. Slice onions very thinly and break into rings.

Whisk together wine, oil and vinegar and stir in onion and garlic. Season with pepper.

Arrange orange slices and onion rings in glass serving bowl, layering with black olives. Pour over dressing and when ready to serve, mix oranges and onions with dressing.

NOTE TO COOK: Either carry salad to party in serving bowl, tightly wrapped, or carry onions, oranges and olives in separate containers and dressing in a fourth container. Arrange at party.

This very pretty salad is the creation of Carrie Lee Nelson.

24 ounces Chinese vermicelli, broken into 6-inch lengths*

1 cup light soy sauce*

½ cup fresh lemon juice

2 tablespoons rice vinegar*

2 tablespoons sugar

4 teaspoons grated fresh ginger

1 tablespoon Oriental sesame oil*

2 teaspoons hot chili oil*

Freshly ground black pepper to taste

3 cups halved cherry tomatoes

¾ cup minced scallions

Place noodles in large bowl; add boiling water. Soak until soft, about 15 minutes. Drain noodles; rinse under cold water; drain well. Set aside.

Combine soy sauce, lemon juice, vinegar, sugar, ginger, sesame oil, chili oil and pepper and stir until sugar dissolves. Just before serving, pour sauce over noodles; toss to mix well. Add tomatoes and scallions. Toss gently and serve at room temperature.

NOTE TO COOK: Prepare noodles and carry to party in covered container. Prepare sauce and carry in separate container. Halve tomatoes and mince scallions and carry each of them in separate containers. At serving time toss and serve from shallow bowl.

* Available at Oriental grocery stores.

Adapted from a recipe Russell Carr uses at the Chelsea Baking Company in New York.

CRUST:

2 cups ground pecans
2 tablespoons brown sugar
1 egg white, beaten until frothy

1 teaspoon powdered ginger
1 teaspoon finely grated lemon rind

TO MAKE CRUST: Mix nuts with brown sugar, egg white, ginger and lemon rind just until mixture is bound together. Press into bottom and sides of 9-inch springform pan.

FILLING:

2 pounds softened cream cheese
¾ cup sugar
4 eggs, lightly beaten
½ cup heavy cream
1 teaspoon vanilla extract
8 ounces ginger preserves

2 teaspoons powdered ginger
1 tablespoon finely grated fresh ginger
Candied ginger minced, for garnish

TO MAKE FILLING: Beat cream cheese and sugar together until smooth and light. Add eggs, cream, vanilla, ginger preserves, powdered ginger and fresh ginger. Mix thoroughly and pour into prepared nut crust.

Bake at 300 degrees for 1 hour and 40 minutes. Cool 1 hour in turned-off oven or overnight. Cool completely before chilling in the refrigerator.

NOTE TO COOK: Carry to party in springform pan along with candied ginger. To serve, remove band from springform. Decorate with candied ginger. Place on serving tray.

CRUST:

4 ounces semisweet chocolate

3 tablespoons unsalted butter

1 cup chopped toasted almonds

¼ teaspoon almond extract

TO MAKE CRUST: Melt chocolate and butter over hot water or very carefully over direct heat. Stir in almonds and extract. Chill until thick enough to spread in 9-inch springform pan. Chill.

FILLING:

6-ounce package semisweet chocolate pieces

1½ pounds cream cheese, at room temperature

1 cup sugar

3 eggs

2 cups sour cream

1 teaspoon vanilla extract

Shaved chocolate for decoration, optional

TO MAKE FILLING: Melt chocolate over hot water or carefully over very low heat. In large bowl beat cream cheese with sugar until fluffy. Add the eggs, one at a time, beating well after each addition. Add sour cream and vanilla and beat.

Combine melted chocolate with ½ cup of batter. Spoon half of the plain cheese mixture into prepared springform. Add spoons of half of the chocolate batter; then add remaining plain batter and finally spoons of the remaining chocolate batter. With a knife draw lines through chocolate into plain batter to marbleize.

Bake at 350 degrees for 1 hour and 10 to 20 minutes. Cool. Then chill for several hours or overnight.

NOTE TO COOK: Carry to party in springform pan. Carry a piece of semisweet chocolate in plastic bag for shavings. To serve, remove band from springform and decorate top of cake with shavings. Place on serving tray.

Oysters with saffron-ginger sauce

Roast turkey with pine nut and rice stuffing
Carrot puree
Cauliflower puree
Spiked cranberry-orange relish

Apple and endive salad with grapefruit dressing

Pumpkin cheesecake in nut crust
Chocolate-pecan-grapefruit tartes

Cooking facilities needed: oven, top of stove   Silverware needed: fork, knives

Two people might want to work on the turkey and its stuffing or two different people might each make one of the Chocolate-Pecan-Grapefruit tartes. Or the person who does not have to cook anything might bring all the wine.

Oysters with saffron-ginger sauce (Sauce R1)

1 pound, 4 ounces fresh ginger

2 teaspoons saffron

3 cups Crème Fraîche (see page 172)

6 cups chicken stock or broth

White pepper to taste

3 dozen shucked oysters, 3 dozen of deepest shells reserved

White wine

1½ to 2 cups finely grated Parmesan cheese

Peel ginger and grate finely. There should be about 3 cups of pulp. Place in cheesecloth and squeeze juice into bowl, yielding about 9 ounces. Add saffron to juice and allow to sit for one hour. This can be prepared a day ahead.

Reduce crème fraîche to 1½ to 2 cups. Pour off any liquid that separates. Reduce stock to 9 tablespoons. Mix with reduced crème fraîche. Add ginger mixture and white pepper to taste. These two steps can be prepared a day ahead.

Poach oysters in white wine to cover, until edges curl, about 2 to 3 minutes. Remove oysters. Nap shells with about 2 tablespoons of crème fraîche sauce. Replace oysters. Sprinkle each with about 2 teaspoons Parmesan cheese. Refrigerate if desired for an hour or two. To serve, broil until bubbly.

NOTE TO COOK: Carry prepared oysters to party in storage container. Broil on baking sheets to serve.

Roast turkey with pine nut and rice stuffing

(Stuffing R1)   (ENOUGH STUFFING FOR 24-POUND TURKEY, ABOUT 16 CUPS)

4½ cups chicken broth

2¼ cups uncooked long-grain rice

6 tablespoons unsalted butter

12 scallions, minced

3 pounds lean ground turkey, chicken or veal

1 cup pine nuts

1½ cups boiling water

½ cup minced fresh parsley

12 juniper berries

3 small bay leaves, very thoroughly crumbled

¾ teaspoon powdered sage

Salt and freshly ground black pepper to taste

2 cups raisins

24-pound dressed, plain turkey (fresh if possible)

Bring broth to boil; stir in rice. Reduce heat to low, cover and simmer until rice is cooked; set aside.

Melt butter in large skillet over medium heat. Add scallions and stir until soft, 2 to 3 minutes. Reduce heat to low. Add ground meat and pine nuts and cook until meat loses its pink color, breaking up meat with fork. Discard excess fat. Stir in rice, boiling water, parsley, juniper berries, bay leaves and sage. Raise heat to medium and cook, stirring occasionally, until all liquid is absorbed. Discard juniper berries. Season stuffing with salt and pepper. Stir in raisins. Refrigerate.

To stuff, follow directions.

ROASTING THE TURKEY: Wash, dry and bring turkey to room temperature. Stuff turkey just before roasting. (Don't roast turkey in slow oven overnight; bacteria can multiply rapidly under such conditions.) Truss the bird. Place any leftover stuffing in casserole; cover and bake.

Place the stuffed, trussed bird on a rack, breast up. Rub with butter and baste every 20 minutes or so.

Aluminum foil may be used as a tent over the bird or placed over the breast and drumsticks toward the end of cooking to keep browned skin from burning.

Allow about 30 minutes after the bird has come from the oven before carving. This allows the juices to "set," producing a juicier bird and making carving easier.

An alternative to this method is roasting the turkey in foil. Some people frown on this, saying that it is not roasting, but steaming. But removing the foil toward the end of the cooking time produces a nicely browned turkey, and if you are in doubt about the juiciness of the bird, this is a good method.

However turkey is cooked, remove stuffing as soon as juices have set.

TIMETABLE FOR ROASTING TURKEY

READY-TO-COOK WEIGHT	APPROXIMATE TOTAL COOKING TIME*
6 to 8 pounds	*3 to 3½ hours*
8 to 12 pounds	*3½ to 4 hours*
12 to 16 pounds	*4 to 5 hours*
16 to 20 pounds	*5 to 6 hours*
20 to 26 pounds	*6 to 6½ hours*

This timetable is based on turkey placed in a preheated 325-degree oven. For unstuffed birds, reduce roasting time by 5 minutes per pound.

If thermometer is not used, test for doneness about 1 hour before timetable indicates. Move drumstick up and down. If the turkey is done, the joint should give readily or break. Or press drumstick meat between fingers; the meat should be very soft.

COOKING TURKEY IN FOIL: Prepare turkey as directed for open roasting. Wrap by placing turkey breast side up in middle of large sheet of heavy-duty aluminum foil. For large birds use two widths of foil.

Brush with butter. Place small pieces of foil over ends of legs, tail and wing tips to prevent puncture. Bring long ends of foil up over breast and overlap 3 inches. Close open ends by folding up foil so drippings will not run into pan. Wrap loosely and do not seal airtight.

Place wrapped turkey breast side up in open shallow roasting pan in oven heated to 450 degrees. Open foil once or twice during cooking to judge doneness. When thigh joint and breast meat begin to soften, fold back foil completely to brown turkey and crisp skin.

TIMETABLE FOR COOKING IN FOIL

READY-TO-COOK WEIGHT	APPROXIMATE TOTAL COOKING TIME*
7 to 9 pounds	*2¼ to 2½ hours*
10 to 13 pounds	*2¾ to 3 hours*
14 to 17 pounds	*3 to 3½ hours*
18 to 21 pounds	*4 to 5 hours*
22 to 26 pounds	*5 to 5½ hours*

* Cooking times can vary even more than an hour. So do watch the bird carefully toward the end of the cooking and every time you baste it.

Carrot puree (RI) (18 SERVINGS)

4 pounds carrots
24 scallions, white part only
¾ pound unsalted butter
1½ cups low-fat or regular milk

Freshly ground black pepper and salt to taste
¾ teaspoon dried thyme
1½ cups toasted slivered almonds

Scrape the carrots and cut into medium slices or slice in food processor. Cook carrots in boiling salted water until just tender, about 5 minutes, depending on thickness of slices. Drain and rinse under cold water to stop cooking. Process with steel blade, combining carrots with scallions, butter and milk, in batches. Season with salt, pepper and thyme. Refrigerate, if desired. To serve, heat through. Place in serving dish and sprinkle with almonds.

NOTE TO COOK: Bring to dinner in heavy-bottomed pot and reheat. Sprinkle with almonds and serve.

Cauliflower puree (RI) (18 SERVINGS)

2 large heads cauliflower
½ pound unsalted butter
2 cups milk, approximately

Freshly ground black pepper, salt, nutmeg and mild Hungarian paprika to taste

Break cauliflower into florets and steam over boiling water or cook in boiling water until barely tender. Drain and run under cold water to stop cooking. Using steel blade, process in food processor in two batches, using half the butter and half the milk for each batch. If mixture is too thick, add a little more milk. Combine and season with salt, pepper, nutmeg and paprika.

This may be prepared ahead and refrigerated. Reheat in top of double boiler over hot water.

NOTE TO COOK: Carry to dinner in double boiler and reheat.

Spiked cranberry-orange relish (R7)

1 pound fresh cranberries	¼ cup orange juice
¾ cup sugar	6 tablespoons Grand Marnier
½ cup water	⅔ cup coarsely chopped pecans

Wash and pick over cranberries for foreign pieces. Combine in heavy saucepan with sugar, water and orange juice. Bring to boil; reduce heat and cook at gentle boil until cranberries have popped. If some remain unpopped, that is all right. If you wait until all of them pop, the cranberries will become too soft. Remove from heat; stir in Grand Marnier. Chill.

A couple of hours before serving, stir in pecans.

NOTE TO COOK: Carry relish mixed with pecans to party either in serving bowl wrapped tightly in plastic or in storage container.

Apple and endive salad with grapefruit dressing
(Dressing R1) (18 SERVINGS)

This is an adaptation of a salad served at Déjà-Vu, a restaurant in Philadelphia.

6 tablespoons Dijon mustard	18 medium Belgian endive
1 cup grapefruit juice	9 well-flavored crisp apples (Granny Smith, MacIntosh, etc.)
½ cup safflower oil	
½ cup soy oil	18 large mint leaves (optional)
Freshly ground black pepper and salt to taste	

To make dressing, whisk the mustard with the grapefruit juice. Whisk in oils until mixture is creamy. Season with salt and pepper. Cut the ends off the endive and wash well. Dry and cut into julienne strips. Core but do not peel the apples. Cut into julienne strips. Mix apples with endive and cover immediately with dressing or apples will darken. Serve salad on individual plates, decorated with mint leaves. Dressing may be prepared a day ahead.

NOTE TO COOK: Prepare dressing at home. Julienne endive. Carry mint, dressing, endive and apples to party in separate containers. At party, core and cut apples; mix with endive and dressing and refrigerate. Serve sprinkled with mint.

FILLING:

4 eggs

3 egg yolks

2½ pounds cream cheese, softened

¾ cup firmly packed dark brown sugar

2 teaspoons ground cinnamon

1 teaspoon ground nutmeg

1 teaspoon ground ginger

¼ teaspoon ground allspice

2½ teaspoons finely grated lemon rind

3 tablespoons flour

1 cup heavy cream

1 tablespoon vanilla extract

1 pound can pumpkin puree

Coarsely grated lemon rind for garnish

TO MAKE FILLING: Lightly beat eggs, egg yolks; add softened cream cheese and sugar and beat until thoroughly mixed. Beat in cinnamon, nutmeg, ginger, allspice, lemon rind and flour. Beat in cream, vanilla and pumpkin.

Pour into nut crust; place pan of hot water in bottom of oven to keep cake from cracking. Bake at 400 degrees for 20 minutes. Reduce heat to 275 degrees and bake 50 to 60 minutes longer. Turn off heat and allow cake to cool overnight in oven for 8 hours. Then chill.

NUT CRUST:

2 cups ground pecans

2 tablespoons brown sugar

1 egg white, beaten until frothy

1 teaspoon powdered ginger

1 teaspoon finely grated lemon rind

TO MAKE CRUST: Mix nuts with brown sugar, egg white, ginger and rind just until mixture is bound together. Press into bottom and a little up the sides of 10-inch springform.

NOTE TO COOK: Refrigerate cake in springform and bring to dinner in the springform. Remove rim before serving and decorate cake with coarsely grated lemon rind.

Check pumpkin can carefully: Do not buy pumpkin pie filling.

Chocolate-pecan-grapefruit tartes (RI)

This refreshing recipe is served at The Inn at Little Washington, Washington, Virginia.

CRUSTS:

5 cups very finely chopped pecans	½ cup melted unsalted butter
⅔ cup sugar	4 ounces semisweet chocolate, melted

TO MAKE CRUST: Mix pecans and sugar together; add melted butter. Press into 2 10-inch pie plates and chill for 30 minutes. Bake at 375 degrees for 10 minutes. Cool to room temperature.

Dribble melted chocolate over cooled shells.

FILLING:

¼ pound unsalted butter	8 eggs, slightly beaten
½ cup heavy cream	2 packages gelatin dissolved in ½ cup grapefruit juice
1⅓ cups fresh grapefruit juice	
1 cup fresh orange juice	Whipped cream, grapefruit segments and grated chocolate for garnish
Grated rind of 4 grapefruits	
1½ cups sugar	

TO MAKE FILLING: Melt butter with cream. Add juices, rind, sugar and eggs and cook over medium-high heat, whisking constantly, until mixture thickens. Strain through fine sieve.

Warm dissolved gelatin over water until clear and add to custard mixture.

When filling cools to room temperature, pour into chocolate-lined crusts. Refrigerate at least 6 hours or overnight.

Decorate with whipped cream, grapefruit segments and chocolate curls.

NOTE TO COOK: Prepare and carry to dinner in pie plates, carefully covered with foil. Do not let foil touch filling. Prepare grapefruit segments ahead and carry in separate container or plastic bag. Bring heavy cream for whipping and a square of semisweet chocolate to make curls.

At dessert time, whip cream and make chocolate curls, using parer. Decorate pies.

Potato cheese pancakes
Sausages
Amaretto applesauce

Sherley's peaches with ginger berry sauce
Giant oatmeal spice cookies

Coffee, tea, wine
Screwdrivers, Mimosas

Cooking facilities needed: top of stove, oven   *Silverware needed: forks*

This menu requires some last-minute cooking.

Potato cheese pancakes

(12 SERVINGS)

These are done easily in food processor.

3 cups coarsely grated sharp white cheddar cheese

3 medium onions, quartered

18 ounces (1 pound, 2 ounces) cream cheese, softened

3 eggs

3 egg yolks

9 tablespoons (½ cup plus 1 tablespoon) flour

¾ cup heavy cream

Salt and freshly ground black pepper to taste

6 pounds potatoes, peeled

Vegetable oil

Grate cheese and combine with quartered onion plus all remaining ingredients but potatoes and oil. Blend mixture with steel blade. Grate potatoes coarsely. Combine with remaining ingredients.

Film large skillet with oil. When almost smoking, spoon in potato mixture, making 3- or 4-inch pancakes about ⅛ inch thick. Cook the pancakes until golden brown on bottom; turn and brown carefully on second side.

Pancakes may be kept warm in single layer in 200-degree oven.

NOTE TO COOK: All the ingredients can be combined, with the exception of the potatoes, the day before. To make the pancakes, peel and grate potatoes and add to batter. Carry batter to party in storage container. Prepare pancakes at party. They can be kept warm in oven for about 20 minutes.

Sausages

Allow one or two sausages per person, depending on the size. Select a variety such as sweet and hot Italian, bratwurst, weisswurst (if you can find them), kielbasa.

Boil or pan-fry, depending on variety.

NOTE TO COOK: Sausages can be prepared at party about 20 minutes before serving and kept warm at low temperature in oven.

Amaretto applesauce (F/R3)   (6 CUPS)

This recipe was created by my daughter, Ann, who loves to experiment in the kitchen.

4 pounds firm cooking apples—
Granny Smith, for example
3 cups pitted Bing cherries*

2 teaspoons cinnamon
½ to 1 cup sugar
½ cup amaretto

Core apples and cut into chunks. Combine with cherries and cinnamon. Cook, covered, until apples are soft, about 35 to 45 minutes. Spoon the mixture into a blender or food processor and blend until smooth. Repeat until all of mixture is pureed. Return to pot with sugar to taste. Boil gently, stirring occasionally, so apples don't stick to bottom of pan, for about 15 minutes, until sauce reduces and thickens a little. After 10 minutes, add amaretto and continue cooking for 5 minutes longer.

Serve warm or cool. Refrigerate or freeze if desired.

NOTE TO COOK: Carry to party in storage container or serving bowl.

* Use fresh cherries in season. It takes about 20 ounces to make 3 cups of pitted cherries. When cherries are no longer in season, use frozen or canned cherries. If using canned cherries, drain off syrup.

Sherley's peaches with ginger berry sauce

(Sauce R1)

Sherley Koteen's contributions to my books are a good luck charm.

2 quarts berries (blue, rasp, huckle, black, black rasp or any combination of the above

1⅓ cups water

Sugar, depending on sweetness of berries. Start with ½ cup for 3 cups juice

1 tablespoon lemon juice, approximately, depending on flavor of berries

4 teaspoons minced fresh ginger

6 wedges peeled peaches (about ¼ inch wide) per serving

1 cup Crème Fraîche (see recipe page 172)

Wash berries and pick over to remove extraneous material and spoiled berries. Combine with water and simmer about 10 minutes, until berries are very soft. Place cooked berries and liquid in a double thickness of cheesecloth and suspend over a pot. (To do this, tie the cheesecloth like a hobo's sack and hang from a long fork, spoon handle or chopstick over pot.) Allow juice to drain from berries for an hour, without squeezing the fruit. (Discard or eat fruit.)

Measure the juice. Adjust seasonings to taste. Stir in ginger. Bring juice to boil; reduce heat and simmer 5 minutes. Cool. Strain out ginger. Refrigerate, if desired.

To serve, return juice to room temperature. Peel peaches, and if they will not be served immediately, sprinkle with lemon juice and mix to be certain all the surfaces are covered. The peaches can be cut up several hours ahead and refrigerated until serving time.

Carefully spoon 3 tablespoons of sauce into center of salad-size plate to create a pool. Arrange peach slices in circular fashion on the sauce. Place a tablespoon of crème fraîche in center and serve.

NOTE TO COOK: Carry sauce to party in tightly covered storage container. Carry crème fraîche in another container and carry peaches, well wrapped, in a third container. Just before serving, arrange individual plates.

A recipe from the Winterthur Point to Point Races from one of the tail-gaters, Harriet Kimmel.

1½ cups sifted flour
  2 teaspoons ground cinnamon
  2 teaspoons ground allspice
1½ teaspoons ground cloves
1½ teaspoons ground ginger
  ½ teaspoon finely ground black pepper
  Pinch salt

½ teaspoon baking soda
½ pound unsalted butter
1 teaspoon vanilla extract
1 cup granulated sugar
1 cup light brown sugar, firmly packed
2 eggs
3 cups quick-cooking rolled oats

Sift the flour with the spices, salt and baking soda and set aside. Cream the butter; add vanilla, white and brown sugars and beat well, until creamy. Add eggs and beat. On low speed of electric mixer beat in sifted dry ingredients. Stir oats in with spoon.

Line two cookie sheets with aluminum foil, shiny side down. Place 10 cookies on each sheet, using ¼ cup of batter for each. Let stand 2 hours before baking. Bake at 375 degrees for 12 to 15 minutes on racks that have been placed on second and third rungs in oven. Reverse sheets once during baking. The cookies should be quite soft when they are done. Cool on racks before removing from sheets.

NOTE TO COOK: Carry to party in storage container. Arrange on serving platter at party.

Baked stuffed papaya

Fruits and vegetables with peanut sauce

Baltimore cheese bread

Whole-wheat blueberry muffins

Benne seed cookies

Coffee, tea, wine

Bloody Marys, Mimosas

No last-minute cooking   Silverware needed: forks

The noncook or cooks for this party can bring the wine, Bloody Marys or Mimosas. Or whatever else the host or hostess decides to serve.

Baked stuffed papaya (R1)   (12 SERVINGS)

½ teaspoon ground coriander seed

1 teaspoon ground cumin

3 cups cottage cheese

3 cups cream cheese

2 tablespoons dry vermouth

2 teaspoons curry powder

6 tablespoons chopped chutney

6 tablespoons golden raisins

1 cup very thinly sliced water chestnuts

6 ripe papayas, cut in half and seeded *

Combine the coriander, cumin, cottage and cream cheeses, vermouth, curry and chutney and mix thoroughly to blend well. Add the raisins and water chestnuts and mix to blend.

Use to fill the seeded papaya halves. Cover tightly and refrigerate.

NOTE TO COOK: To carry to party, wrap tightly with plastic wrap on serving dish or carry in storage container and arrange on serving dish at party.

* It is often difficult to find ripe papayas. Given four to five days, those with a blush of yellow on them already will ripen. They are ripe when they are yellow all over and yield to slight pressure.

Fruits and vegetables with peanut sauce

½ cup Oriental sesame paste*

2 tablespoons peanut oil

1 teaspoon hot chili oil

4 tablespoons hot water

2 tablespoons imported Chinese or Japanese soy sauce

4 tablespoons red wine vinegar

2 tablespoons sesame oil

2 small ripe pineapples or one very large pineapple

8 small Kirby cucumbers or 4 medium regular cucumbers

2 ripe medium cantaloupes

½ pound fresh spinach

2 small bunches scallions

Combine sesame paste, peanut and chili oils and hot water and beat to blend. Add soy sauce, vinegar and sesame oil and beat thoroughly.

Peel and core the pineapples, slice and cut into bite-size wedges. If using the small Kirby cucumbers, simply scrub, cut off ends but do not peel. If using the regular waxed cucumbers, they must be peeled. Cut the Kirbys into ½-inch slices. Cut the regular cucumbers in half lengthwise and then into ½-inch slices. Peel the melons and seed. Cut into bite-size wedges.

Remove the tough stems from the spinach leaves and wash; drain dry on paper toweling. Thinly slice the scallions.

Refrigerate the sauce in a container with a tight-fitting lid. Refrigerate each of the fruits and vegetables in a separate container (the spinach and scallions can be put in plastic bags).

To serve, cover a shallow serving dish with the spinach leaves and arrange the fruit in circles. Sprinkle with scallions and drizzle peanut sauce over all.

NOTE TO COOK: Carry to party in individual containers and arrange at party or arrange fruits and vegetables on platter at home but carry sauce separately. Stir well before pouring over fruits and vegetables just before serving.

* Oriental sesame paste is made with toasted sesame seeds; others are not. It has a more intense, more interesting flavor, so is recommended. If you cannot find it, use Middle Eastern sesame paste called tahini.

This cheese bread was created by Dean Kolstad, the original owner of Ms Desserts, one of the most popular food booths at Baltimore's Harborplace.

¼ cup plus 1 teaspoon sugar
1 package active dry yeast
2 eggs
1 cup milk
½ cup unsalted butter, melted and cooled to room temperature

1 teaspoon salt
About 5 cups unbleached flour
1 pound Svenbo, Jarlsberg or Swiss cheese, grated (4 cups)

GLAZE:

1 egg, lightly beaten

In a small bowl stir 1 teaspoon sugar into 3 tablespoons warm water; stir in yeast and set aside until dissolved.

In large bowl, lightly beat eggs. Mix in remaining sugar, milk, butter and salt. Blend in the yeast mixture and then stir in 2 cups of flour to make a dough. Stir in another 1½ cups flour, turn the dough onto a work surface and knead in enough of the remaining flour to make a soft, smooth dough. Knead the dough about 15 minutes more, or until it is smooth and satiny.

Place dough in lightly oiled bowl, turn it to lightly grease the surface, cover with a tea towel and allow it to rise in a warm place until double in bulk, about 1½ hours.

Thoroughly grease a 9-inch pie pan. Punch down dough and roll it into a 16-inch round. Center dough in pie pan, pressing it snugly against the edges of the pan and allowing the excess to hang over. Mound the cheese in the center and fold and pleat the dough into a turban shape by gathering it into 6 or 7 equally spaced folds, stretching the dough slightly as you draw each pleat over the filling. Hold the ends of the dough in your hand, twist them together tightly on top. Glaze the surface by brushing it with the lightly beaten egg. Set it aside in a warm place and let it rise until double in bulk, about 45 minutes.

Bake bread at 325 degrees in center of oven for about 50 minutes, or until top is golden brown and bread sounds hollow when lightly tapped on the side. Cool for 15 minutes, remove from pan and let rest another 30 minutes before slicing into wedges and serving.

NOTE TO COOK: This can be prepared ahead. Just warm it at 300 degrees for about 5 minutes before serving. If you live near the party you are bringing it to, warm it at home; wrap well in aluminum foil and transport. It looks nice on a square or round cutting board.

1¾ cups whole-wheat flour
½ teaspoon salt
½ cup sugar
2 teaspoons baking powder
2 eggs

¼ cup melted unsalted butter
¾ cup plain yogurt
1½ cups fresh or dry-pack frozen blueberries

Combine flour, salt, sugar and baking powder. Beat eggs; add butter and yogurt and stir. Combine liquid ingredients with dry ingredients, stirring only long enough to moisten. Fold in blueberries.

Fill greased muffin tins two-thirds full and bake at 400 degrees for 15 to 20 minutes, or until muffins are golden brown.

To make 6 miniature loaves 4 × 2 × 1½ inches, bake 30 to 35 minutes. Serve with butter or cream cheese.

These muffins can be frozen or prepared a day ahead and wrapped tightly, stored at room temperature, if desired, but they should be reheated at 300 degrees for 5 minutes before serving.

NOTE TO COOK: Don't forget to bring the butter or cream cheese along with the muffins.

The muffins can be carried in the tins in which they were baked and warmed.

Benne is the word for sesame that the slaves brought with them from Africa. The name is still used in the South, where you will find benne seed wafers as well as cookies.

12 tablespoons unsalted butter	½ teaspoon baking powder
1 cup brown sugar	1 teaspoon vanilla extract
1 egg	¾ cup toasted sesame seeds
1 cup flour	

Cream butter until soft. Gradually beat in sugar until mixture is soft and fluffy. Beat in egg until smooth. Combine flour and baking powder and stir into creamed batter. Add vanilla and sesame seeds and mix well.

Onto greased cookie sheets drop by teaspoonfuls about 1½ inches apart. Bake at 325 degrees 12 to 15 minutes, then remove immediately from sheets. If cookies harden before they are removed, return to oven to soften.

Store in tightly covered container or freeze.

NOTE TO COOK: Five dozen cookies are more than you will need for twelve people. But they are always nice to have and keep well, especially in the freezer. They are ready almost at a moment's notice because they defrost quickly.

COOPERATIVE DINNERS— RECIPES BY CATEGORIES

Keep in mind that if you use these recipes separate from the menus of which they are part, you will have to adjust the serving size for some of them.

APPETIZERS

MAIN DISHES

SALADS

SIDE DISHES

BREADS

DESSERTS

INDEX

About the Author

Marian Burros is the award-winning food critic of *The New York Times*. She has also been an Emmy recipient for her consumer reporting on NBC-TV in Washington, D.C., and is the author of a number of well-known cookbooks, including *Elegant but Easy* and two *New York Times* best sellers, *Pure & Simple* and *Keep It Simple*. Marian, who jogs five miles a day to counteract the demands of her job, is a frequent contributor to many magazines. She has been writing about food for more than twenty years.